CANADA IS NOT
A REAL COUNTRY

Canada Is Not a Real Country

Thomas Schnurmacher

ECW PRESS

CANADIAN CATALOGUING IN PUBLICATION DATA

Schnurmacher, Thomas
Canada is not a real country

ISBN 1-55022-290-2

1. Quebec (Province) — Politics and
government — 1960– 2. Canada — English-French
relations. 3. Federal-provincial relations —
Quebec (Province). 4. Canada — Constitutional
law — Amendments. 5. Quebec Liberal Party.
6. Parti quebecois. I. Title.

FC2925.9.S4S36 1996   971.4´04   C96-990092-9
FI053.2.S36 1996

Design and imaging by ECW Type & Art, Oakville, Ontario.
Printed by Imprimerie Québecor L'Eclaireur, Beauceville, Québec.

Distributed in Canada by General Distribution Services,
30 Lesmill Road, Don Mills, Ontario M3B 2T6.

Published by ECW PRESS,
2120 Queen Street East, Suite 200,
Toronto, Ontario M4E 1E2
www.ecw.ca/press

ACKNOWLEDGEMENTS

The title of this book was inspired by a mean-spirited remark by Quebec Premier Lucien Bouchard, but it is dedicated to the twenty-eight million people who love this great country.

It is dedicated to all federalists, especially French Canadian federalists who had the courage to stand up to the separatist orthodoxy and mythology.

They remain proud of their heritage of building this great country. They refuse to tell their grandchildren that they voted to destroy Canada in the name of a narrow-minded ethnocentric vision that continues to undermine the great province of Quebec.

This book is dedicated to the native peoples, the so-called ethnics, and to all others who must continue to fight for the only true democracy that has any meaning — a democracy where no government is above the rule of law.

The real inspiration for this book is the strength and character of the Canadian people who will not stand idly by while their country is destroyed in the name of an ethnic nationalism that belongs to the past — not the future.

Last, but not least, this book is dedicated to all the lobsters who are too wise to jump into the PQ pot.

I would like to thank all the helpful and talented people at ECW PRESS who helped this book to become a reality. Special kudos to my researcher and editing assistant, Mark Lurie, for his intelligence and dedication, not to mention the devil's advocate role that he filled so well. A tip of the hat to the ubiquitous Stanley Grunfeld for proofreading the book before it went to print and offering many valuable suggestions.

Thank you as well to my parents, Michael and Olga, and my sister, Cynthia, who were graciously patient with me despite all the time I spent on the book. Special thanks also to good friends like H.W. Aylmer, Francine Goldberg, Richard Dermer, Roni and Ed Blanshay, Mireille and Marika Coulourides, Joanne Sternthal, Rochelle Lach, Rebecca Eichler, Susan Davis, Chabad and Rabbi Ronnie Fine as well as Marty O'Rourke from Vancouver who told me that I should have written this book years ago.

I would also like to thank Josée Legault, who will probably disagree with every word in this book but who remains a friend nonetheless.

A special note of thanks to CJAD radio program director Steve Kowch who always knows how to get me revved up. And to my listeners — thank you for keeping me on my toes.

TABLE OF CONTENTS

INTRODUCTION

On January 27, 1996, Quebec premier Lucien Bouchard declared, "Canada is not a real country."

Where on earth would he get such an idea?

Well, truth be told, Bouchard doesn't think that Canada is a real country because Canada, quite frankly, does not *act* like a real country.

If it did, it would not continue to put up with the constant threats from separatists to deprive their fellow citizens of the country they love.

According to a report published in June 1996 by the C.D. Howe Institute, there is not a single constitution in the entire world that allows a region seeking independence from a country to hold its own referendum. Read the previous sentence again. *Not a single country in the entire world would put up with this ridiculous situation of having the people who want to break it up set out the rules for how they plan to do it.*

The Howe report looked at 160 constitutions from around the world and found that only seven countries have provisions in their constitutions to conduct referendums on splitting up the state. Those seven countries are Singapore, Senegal, Mali, Congo, Gabon, Panama, and Zaire. But not a single country — not one anywhere in the world — is stupid enough to grant one of its regions the legal authority to draft the wording of the question, set the date, and count the vote all on its own.

The only country in the world to put up with such nonsense is Canada.

Only in Canada? What a pity indeed.

No wonder Lucien Bouchard is convinced that Canada is not a real country. But that is how he puts it kindly. For if Canada does not go along like a lamb to the slaughterhouse, Bouchard says that Canada is a "prison."

Bouchard's shameless disdain for this country goes way back. He used to show off his Parti Québécois membership card at lavish diplomatic parties in Paris while the federal government was paying his fat salary as Canada's ambassador to France in the late 1980s.

If not for former prime minister Brian Mulroney, Bouchard would probably still be plying his trade as a unilingual small-town lawyer in Lac-St-Jean. It was Mulroney who plucked Bouchard from relative obscurity. Bouchard repaid the favour by stabbing his best friend in the back. Nor did he hesitate for a moment to humiliate Jacques Parizeau, his predecessor as leader of the Parti Québécois, by publicly shoving him aside in the midst of the last referendum battle.

Mila Mulroney, showing better instincts than her husband, never trusted Bouchard. After the betrayal, Mulroney's loathing of his former friend became so intense that the two men still do not speak. According to Peter C. Newman, the hatred goes so deep that Mulroney has left instructions that, in case Bouchard shows up at his funeral, the service is to be stopped until Bouchard is thrown out.

Lucien Bouchard is the man who rushed his pregnant wife, Audrey Best, to a hospital across the bridge from Ottawa into Hull, so as to make sure that his son would be born on Quebec soil. This mawkish display of nationalism prompted members of Ottawa's press corps to refer to the Bouchard baby as "Le P'tit Oui."

Bouchard promised his own wife that he would quit politics after the October 30 referendum. Not only did he manage to renege on that promise, but he used his much-touted charisma to convince her that she had gone along with his decision. While Lucien Bouchard was pretending to consult his wife on the decision, many Canadians were convinced that the very future of the greatest country in the world suddenly hinged on the whim of a former American stewardess!

Canada had clearly gone mad. Fortunately, though, this country is much more solid than it appears to be if one judges by its pathetic political leadership.

After the narrow victory for the No side, the federal government became paralyzed with a bad case of post-traumatic stress syndrome. In the immediate aftermath of the referendum, Canadians, who realized how close they had just come to the total breakup of the country, were clearly in a state of shock. In those heady days of November, many Canadians were so freaked out by what had just happened that they were ready to do *anything*. Never mind granting Quebec distinct society status in the Constitution — at that point, they would have literally agreed to sell Quebec anglophones into bondage, if only Quebec promised not to leave.

Fortunately, cooler heads prevailed.

The future of this country will not be decided by Lucien Bouchard and Audrey Best. The future of this country must be decided within the rule of law, and it must be decided by all Canadians.

But why did Lucien Bouchard think he could get away with saying that Canada is not a real country?

Because the federal government — let's face it — had not been acting like one until May 1996, when it finally publicly took sides in the Guy Bertrand court challenge to Bouchard's threat of a unilateral declaration of independence. We had a prime minister who refused to stand up for the very territorial integrity of Canada. We had a justice minister who said that the rule of law was a mere technicality. We had members of the anglophone "lamb lobby" in Quebec — federalists who passively accept separatist mythology — come out with the preposterous notion that the democratic will of the people as expressed in a referendum is more important than any law.

This is madness.

What if the democratic will of the people of Quebec as expressed in a referendum was to stop paying any taxes to Ottawa and turn all other Canadians into their slaves? We would not put up with that. So why on earth would we put up with the ridiculous notion that less than half the population of Quebec has the right to radically alter the future of twenty-eight million other Canadians, who are expected to shut up and keep quiet while all of this is going on?

In true banana republic style, Quebec's chief electoral officer, using a former Quebec chief justice as a cover, came to the preposterous conclusion that, even though thousands of votes had been stolen during the October referendum, there had been no "national" conspiracy. His so-called investigation looked at a *sampling* of ballots in 290 ballot boxes, leaving 22,000 boxes untouched. Monty Python would have been pleased.

The more one looks at the total lack of leadership that has been the hallmark of the Canadian government in the 1990s, the more one can understand why Lucien Bouchard would think that Canada is not a real country.

Yet the separatists' reasoning is seriously flawed.

When Charles Gibson interviewed Lucien Bouchard on *Good Morning America*, he asked him the obvious question: Canada is such a stable country, so why on earth would you want to break it apart? Bouchard replied that it is because Canada doesn't recognize Quebec as a nation, and, secondly, because Canada invades some of Quebec's provincial jurisdictions.

What jurisdictions exactly is he talking about? The federal government virtually never imposes its will on Quebec, and routinely goes along with blatant violations of its own Constitution in order to placate nationalists. And even if Bouchard's complaint were true — which it isn't — it would still not be reason enough to break up a country.

Secondly, French Canadians may be considered a nation, but Quebec itself is not a nation, for one very simple reason. There are one million French Canadians living outside Quebec, and there are one million Quebec citizens who are not French Canadian. Confederation in 1867 was the creation of a political nation of English Canadians and French Canadians who worked together to build the great land that they had stolen from the native peoples.

Personally, I am extremely proud to be part of the great Canadian nation, a nation built by English Canadians, French Canadians, new Canadians, and the native peoples. I have no desire to be deprived of my rights as a Canadian citizen as guaranteed by the Charter of Rights. And there are millions of other loyal Canadians living in Quebec who would agree with me that they have no intention of being hijacked from one jurisdiction to another against their will just because some of our confrères are determined to live in a xenophobic, ethnocentric state where they can pass racist language laws to their hearts' content.

Canada is a great, pluralistic democracy that has acted as a buffer zone to protect the French language and culture, and to prevent Quebec from becoming another Louisiana. The great tragedy of this country is that so damn few of our so-called federalist politicians have ever bothered to bring that up. We continue to fight on the separatist playing field when we say that we have to work hard to make Quebecers feel more at home in Canada. We have been doing that for the past thirty years and it has not worked. The more we appease, the more we whet the separatist appetite for more.

To say that Quebecers do not feel at home in Canada is part of the nationalist mantra. But it is absolutely not true. The prime minister of this country is a Quebecer. Every single member of the official opposition is a Quebecer. So is the chief justice of the Supreme Court.

The list goes on and on. Add the finance minister, the labour minister, the chief clerk of the Privy Council, the ambassador to Washington, the governor general. How's that for making Quebecers feel at home? Quebecers run not only Quebec, but all of Canada — and it is still not enough.

Can you imagine an anglophone as premier of Quebec? Of course not. But Canadians keep electing Quebecers to be prime minister: Pierre Trudeau, Brian Mulroney, Jean Chrétien. Prime ministers who are not from Quebec, such as Joe Clark, John Turner, and Kim Campbell, are merely footnotes to history.

Trudeau gave us official bilingualism, added billions to the debt, created French power in Ottawa, and devised an energy policy that almost destroyed the West.

Brian Mulroney gave us Meech Lake, Charlottetown, and Lucien Bouchard. He said that the Canadian Constitution was not worth the paper it was written on. Mulroney, who was having Bouchard write his speeches, spent his entire career as prime minister undermining the Canadian federation by validating the separatist argument that Quebec had been humiliated during the patriation of the Constitution in 1982. From the moment Mulroney made a pact with the separatists to help get himself elected, Quebec nationalists were not the only ones who were saying that they had been humiliated. They now had a Canadian prime minister validating their argument.

Jean Chrétien gave us federal inaction and unparalleled moral cowardice that led us to the brink of disaster. A few days before the last referendum, we were treated to the sight of the prime minister of this country *begging* on television for Quebecers to vote No. What a low point in the history of a great country when the prime minister is reduced to begging. A pathetic performance.

And in a twisted idea of what constitutes fair play, Chrétien gives equal time to the man who wants to tear Canada apart! Can you imagine the president of France giving equal television time to the leader of the Corsican separatist movement? Can you imagine the prime ministers of Great Britain or Italy offering equal time to their own separatist movements?

Imagine a bank manager making a speech to his employees on the rules, regulations, and policies of the bank. He spells out his vision for what the bank stands for and where he would like to take the bank in the future. Then, after his employees applaud, he gives the floor to the robber holding up the bank. He tells him, "Now *you* have an equal opportunity to put forth your vision of how you view the bank and its operations."

Only in Canada.

If the prime minister of Canada is stupid enough to give separatism equal time, Lucien Bouchard is not about to look a gift horse in the mouth. Bouchard rises to the occasion by delivering two different speeches. The one in English is sophisticated, eloquent, and diplomatic. The one in French is the fire and brimstone of a campaigning demagogue in full frenzy. Bouchard goes so far as to reproduce the tacky cover of a fourteen-year-old cheap tabloid showing Trudeau and Chrétien laughing together after the patriation of the Constitution. Chrétien, trying to be a gentleman, never explains what he and Trudeau were laughing about in the picture, so the photo enters the canon of mythology that Jean Chrétien was laughing at Quebec.

Chrétien is still so scared of Bouchard and the separatists that he is now busy trying to peddle distinct society status for Quebec when he knows full well that it would only serve to further increase the desire for independence. Former premier Jacques Parizeau once told journalist Barbara Frum that if Quebec were to be given distinct society status, he would use it to leave Canada via the front door.

Just look up the word "distinct" in the dictionary. It means "separate." That's why nationalists invented the term! Even without distinct society, Quebec has still managed to completely flout the Constitution in both letter and spirit. English and French are the official languages of Canada. But in Quebec, the only official language is French.

It is still not enough.

Ontario now has more French schools than Quebec has English schools. Quebec has to close hospitals and charge the elderly for their medication, but the government manages to muster $215,000 for a statue of Charles de Gaulle, not to mention $5 million for language "inspectors," also known as tongue troopers, even though the vast majority of Quebecers do not like the idea that government officials can have the right to rifle through a company's papers and computer records on a language complaint that can be launched by anyone from a rival company to a disgruntled employee.

The federal government turns a blind eye as Canadian citizens who live in Quebec continue to be deprived of rights enjoyed by other Canadians in the rest of the country, but it is still not enough. No matter what Canada does, it will never be enough. Staunch Quebec nationalists do not *want* to feel at home in Canada. They want to have their own country. Take their word for it: they mean it.

Soft nationalists, by the hundreds of thousands, are ready

to vote Yes because they are under the illusion that they will get a better deal out of Canada. And, frankly, it is the existence of this group that keeps the threat of separation alive. These are the people who are capable of being persuaded away from voting with the separatists, yet thus far the federal government has been doing everything *wrong*. They cater to the soft nationalists' whimsical demands, even though they know that meeting these demands is a) impossible, and b) essentially a way of guaranteeing that separation occurs.

Out of respect for these people, and for all Canadians who love their country, the federal government must deal with the soft nationalists as adults. When the government explains via contingency legislation that the evolving federalism of Canada is the best deal they are ever going to get, they will start returning to the federalist fold for one very good reason. Soft nationalists do not want to risk going it completely alone and isolated. That's why they are called soft nationalists. They wouldn't mind having their own country, provided there is no risk at all and provided they would not have to face a substantially reduced standard of living. Nor are these soft nationalists particularly thrilled at the prospect of dealing with the Cree and the Inuit, millions of restless federalists, and the spectre of partition.

We must stop trying to fix Canada to appease separatists who will never be appeased. Canada may have problems, but it is not broken. As an immigrant who fled to Canada from Communist Hungary with my parents at the age of five, I can tell you I would rather live with the problems of Canada than the problems of any other country in the world.

Yet I wish the leaders of this great country would be more assertive. The United States and France are both great democracies, but neither one of them is stupid enough to tolerate any attempt to break up the country. In France, it is against the law to have a referendum on secession. The Basques and the Bretons can complain all they like, but they will never be allowed to destroy France. Nor is there much chance that you will ever see the prime minister of France posing with the leader of the Corsican separatists for a photo opportunity while they chat about their golf game.

The breakup of Canada is not a tea party. It would be a great tragedy that would devastate millions of Canadians and create a political upheaval that would affect the lives of every one of us. And for what purpose? To satisfy a xenophobic nationalist movement that is determined to promote the rights of a French-speaking collectivity over individual rights.

The rest of the world is watching and they simply do not understand. They have never before witnessed a great country that seems to be so unconcerned that it could be broken up based on the whim of one segment of its population, led by a charismatic leader whose main talent is spewing rhetoric designed to whip up popular indignation at any humiliation, real or otherwise.

And the Canadian government, aided and abetted by appeasement-worshipping members of the lamb lobby, just keeps playing along.

The separatist plan to break up Canada in order to create a French republic in North America displays an arrogance that is astonishing. If there is a 50-percent-plus-one Yes vote in a referendum, that is all it takes to break up Canada. The wishes, hopes, and dreams of the 50 percent minus one who voted No mean nothing. The opinion of the rest of Canada means nothing. The laws of Canada mean nothing. The Constitution means nothing. Voter fraud means nothing. Asking a trick question to fool as many voters as possible into the trap of outright separation means nothing.

In the event of a Yes vote, the separatists would engage in the largest land grab in recent world history. They would redraw the map of Canada, change its borders and split it apart. And they actually have the chutzpah to suggest that, once they have established a foreign country where the province of Quebec used to be, they will then sit down to establish a political and economic union with the country they have just destroyed. Amazingly, the separatists fully expect the rest of Canada to just shut up and keep quiet while they go about their business of breaking up the country. But, even more amazing, they are getting their way.

The federal government does precious little about the separatist movement, partly because the government is run in large part by French Canadians who do not like the idea of being called traitors or *vendus* by their fellow Quebecers. The federal government allows the separatists to do whatever they like because it is afraid of even saying, much less doing, anything that might offend the nationalists. It fears that anything that Canada might actually do to protect itself and the interests of loyal Canadians would immediately be portrayed as a provocation by an outraged Lucien Bouchard. The federal government is absolutely terrified by the premier of Quebec.

The separatists know this, and, like any successful political organization, they exploit it to their maximum advantage. They depict the road to independence as an effortless cakewalk that will solve every problem, and this rosy picture goes uncountered by a federal government that is as paralyzed as a deer gazing into the headlights.

It never ceases to amaze me how the Canadian government continues to let the separatists run the show and set the terms of the debate.

You don't believe me? Here are a half-dozen examples of how, when it comes to the proposed breakup of Canada, it is the separatists who are setting the agenda while your federal government stands by and does nothing.

Six Ways the Separatists Control the Agenda

1. The separatists choose the number of referendums.
According to Lucien Bouchard, the Parti Québécois will hold as many referendums as it takes — five, six, seven, or possibly more. They will hold as many as they like until the people of Quebec give them the answer that they want to hear.

And what will happen once they get the vote they've been looking for? According to the twisted "democratic" logic of the separatist movement, a vote of 50 percent plus one is final *only* if it is a Yes. A Yes vote means Quebec will become an independent country; a No vote means there will be another referendum.

Since a Yes vote settles everything and a No vote settles nothing, the entire game is rigged in such a manner that it is absolutely impossible for the federalist side to win. The separatists have successfully tricked Canada into playing their game of "Heads we win, tails you lose."

2. The separatists choose the date of the referendum.
When will we have the next referendum? Whenever Lucien Bouchard feels like having it. But you can be sure it won't be an arbitrary decision. While he can threaten to have one whenever he is in the mood, he will actually go through with his threat whenever the polls tell him that he will be successful in whipping the population into an anti-Canada frenzy over yet another perceived slight or humiliation.

In 1990, Pierre Bourgault, now an adviser to the Parti Québécois, wrote a "manifesto for an independent Quebec," entitled *Now or Never!* Yet, as he admitted in the book's introduction, he didn't really mean that the issue would be laid to rest if the people didn't vote to separate "now."

"I don't like that expression very much," he wrote of his own book's title. "There is something definitive about it that doesn't correspond to historical movements and the moods of a nation."

In other words, for the separatists, it's really "Now, or Later."

3. The separatists choose the question.

Why don't the separatists ask the people of Quebec a simple, honest question such as, "Do you want Quebec to separate from Canada?" or "Do you want Quebec to become an independent country?" Because, despite generations of anti-Canada propaganda and the vilification of Ottawa, they recognize that the overwhelming majority of Quebecers remain profoundly attached to Canada.

Most Quebecers know full well that outright separation would be an unmitigated disaster. That's why an imaginary partnership with Canada has to be thrown into the question. The Yes side fared as well as it did the last time because it brilliantly suggested a partnership with Canada. It provided an insurance policy and safety net to reassure those soft nationalists who were afraid of out-and-out separation. Lucien Bouchard assured Quebecers that such a partnership was inevitable. Many Quebecers believed him, especially when they noticed that the prime minister of Canada said nothing to contradict that notion.

The separatists are no fools. In future referendums, they will once again take full advantage of the federal government's fear of speaking up, and will again concoct a trick question designed to reassure as many people as possible that there is absolutely nothing to lose and everything to gain if they vote Yes. Lucien Bouchard will reassure everyone that there is no risk in voting Yes. He will tell Quebecers that the least they will get is a much better deal from Canada, or, better yet, full independence involving a partnership with Canada to cushion the blow.

For this preposterous scenario to be taken seriously, it is

essential for the Canadian government to cooperate by keeping quiet and silencing the voices of anyone who might scream that the emperor is stark naked.

4. The separatists set the rules for the referendum.

By effectively limiting the debate to the hardline nationalist leader of the Yes forces and the soft nationalist leader of the No forces in Quebec, the separatists can stifle any real debate on the all-important issue of territorial integrity, which is the one fly in the separatist ointment. They strive to create the impression that Canadians from outside Quebec are foreigners who have no say in a process designed to break their own country apart.

The Parti Québécois is so taken with its own sense of self-importance that it feels it can pass laws that go beyond its own borders.

As a Canadian, you take it for granted that you have the right to free speech and freedom of assembly. And you do have those rights, most of the time. Except, of course, when the Parti Québécois is having a referendum on breaking up your country. In that case, it is illegal for you to rent a bus to travel to Quebec without registering your expenses with Quebec officials affiliated with the nationalist Yes side or the nationalist No side.

This couldn't have happened the last time, you say? It did happen. You just weren't paying attention, and neither was your federal government.

5. The separatists decide which laws they will obey.

Nationalist politicians have clearly indicated that Quebec is above the law when it comes to secession. While all other Canadians have to deal with an amending formula to make any major changes to the Canadian Constitution, not so for Quebec. They have decided that a solemn declaration in the National Assembly after a trick question in a rigged referendum is all it takes to throw the Canadian Constitution in the trash can.

How's that for an amending formula!

6. The separatists decide what constitutes voter fraud.
The chief electoral officer for the Parti Québécois is Pierre F. Côté, who was a close friend of the late René Lévesque. And — get this — he cannot be fired because he was appointed for life!

When he first hears about allegations of voter fraud, he doesn't want to do anything about it. When he finally looks into the matter, he checks only 290 boxes out of 22,361. He leaves more than 22,000 boxes untouched. And even of the 290 he did peek at, he only looked at a *sample* of those boxes, so he doesn't know the exact number of votes that were stolen.

Côté was more concerned with bus rentals by Ontario college students than with blatant voter fraud.

I am not making this up.

Côté is the chief electoral officer, so he can look into as many boxes as he wants, but he won't. Why not? Because he knows what he'll find, that's why not.

Thousands of Quebec voters protested the voter fraud outside Premier Lucien Bouchard's office. When asked about the allegations by an American interviewer, Bouchard dismissed the protests as just a lot of noise.

Oh? Consider the facts: There were 86,000 spoiled ballots. And the Yes side lost the referendum by only 50,000 votes. Since the separatists were only 50,000 votes away from winning, you'd think they would have demanded an immediate judicial recount. The stakes were very high — having their own country was in the balance — so it does seem passing strange that they never bothered to ask for a recount.

Unless, of course, they knew full well that something was going on.

What has the prime minister of Canada done to come to the aid of Canadian citizens whose votes have been stolen? Absolutely nothing. It is clear that thousands of Canadians have been illegally deprived of a vote, a situation that might have cost them their country, but as far as Pierre F. Côté and Lucien Bouchard are concerned, the investigation is over. The prime minister does nothing. The premier does nothing. And to think we have the gall to send election observers to Haiti!

Canada's Deafening Silence

To think we have gone along with all this nonsense! No wonder Lucien Bouchard thinks that this is not a real country. What other country would allow the leader of a party that wants to break the country apart to become the leader of the opposition? What other country on earth would allow itself to be broken apart based on the vote of 10 percent of its population?

Twenty-eight million Canadians are very proud of this country. Less than three million want to break it up. For some time now, this country has been living under the tyranny of a minority.

But let's not blame the separatists for this state of affairs. They want to create a French state in North America, and if they have to destroy Canada in order to achieve their goal, they couldn't care less. As we approach the 130th anniversary of Confederation, Canada remains a magnificent country that is the envy of the world. The separatists want to break up this country to create their own country. That's their very *raison d'être*. That's their job.

But it isn't easy to destroy such a great country, especially when the majority of Quebecers have always felt a very strong attachment to Canada. It is no accident that the separatists continued to promise Canadian citizenship, Canadian passports, the Canadian dollar, and even a partnership with Canada as part of their last referendum campaign.

The separatists have been successful in convincing Quebecers that they can indeed have their cake and eat it too. Thanks to the federal government's silence about the rule of law and the true consequences of separation, the separatists were never even contradicted as they went about their business of selling the idea of sovereignty combined with the reassuring insurance policy and safety net of a partnership with the rest of a gullible Canada.

Even when it comes to the Canadian military, it is the separatists who set the rules and the federal government just goes along. Bloc Québécois MP Jean-Marc Jacob sends faxes to military bases urging soldiers to transfer their loyalty to the new country of Quebec immediately after a Yes vote. He does this even before Quebec is recognized as an independent country. This letter is sent out on the stationery of the leader of the opposition.

Once again, the separatists could not do it alone. They needed the federal government to cooperate. And they weren't disappointed. First of all, the federal Liberals try to cover it up. When that doesn't work, they agree to discuss the situation in a committee hearing, but they refuse any discussion of sedition. They refuse to call military witnesses. They clear Jean-Marc Jacob of contempt of Parliament.

The Liberals even refuse to set up guidelines dealing with political interference in the Canadian military.

Jean-Marc Jacob states that, if necessary, he will provide the names of the high-ranking Canadian army officials with whom he discussed the creation of a Quebec army. The lying Liberals do not want the people of Canada to know about any of this. They certainly don't want Canadians knowing that the Canadian armed forces have staunch separatists in high-ranking positions. The federal government does not want the people of Canada to find out about that because the people of Canada might actually want their government to *do something* about it.

Don't blame Mr. Jacob, though. He was merely doing his job. And he was doing it openly. Nothing hidden. Open discussions with high-ranking soldiers. Faxes urging soldiers to switch loyalty in full public display at army barracks in Quebec. Mr. Jacob is a man who works hard to achieve his goal. He wants to have an independent country of Quebec and he knows that such a country will need to have an army — especially when it is a country that is being formed against the wishes of half of its population. A new country trying to assert its borders against the wishes of millions of people would *most certainly* need an army. The Cree and the Inuit have democratically expressed their will to stay in Canada to the tune of 95 percent. A new country trying to force these people from one jurisdiction to another against their will would *definitely* need an army.

Mr. Jacob knows this, and that's why he sent out that letter the last time. And the message he got from the federal Liberals is crystal clear: What he did was not treason. It was not sedition. It was not even contempt of Parliament. *It was no big deal!* So what does he care? He did it the last time and, as he told me on my CJAD open-line talk show, he would do it again.

It is the basic premise of this book that the separatists cannot do it alone. They cannot achieve their goal without the cooperation of so-called federalists who have undermined Canada at every turn.

Brian Mulroney said the Constitution of Canada was not worth the paper it was written on. This not only undermined the Canadian federation, but it simultaneously confirmed the separatist vision of having been victimized by "English Canada."

Failed politicians like former prime minister Joe Clark, former NDP chief Ed Broadbent, and former Ontario premiers Bob Rae and David Peterson are the acolytes of appeasement. Not content with their past failures, they continue to threaten Canadians with the demise of this country unless we continue the thoroughly discredited policy of appeasing Quebec. With every utterance, they validate the arguments of the separatists that somehow Canada is just not good enough for Quebec.

And, of course, they all take their cue from the "official" voice for federalism in Quebec, the leader of the provincial Liberal Party, Daniel Johnson. What they don't realize, though, is that half of the population of Quebec did not vote No during the last referendum because they wanted more concessions from Ottawa. Half the population of Quebec voted No because they want to stay in Canada. They voted No not because of Daniel Johnson, but in spite of him.

This country was saved on October 30 by Quebec federalists who love Canada a lot more than they like Daniel Johnson, a man who has, amazingly, been hailed as the most federalist leader in the history of the Quebec Liberal Party. This is a man who believes that Quebec can ignore the Canadian Constitution and unilaterally declare its independence. When asked if a 50-percent-plus-one vote in a Quebec referendum was enough to break up Canada, Johnson replied, "A win is a win." On the subject of partition, Johnson has declared that the borders of Quebec cannot be touched, no matter what. But he is not nearly as concerned about the borders of Canada.

The list of federalists who think that Canada's future hinges on the continued appeasement of Quebec nationalists goes on. The president of the Council for Canadian Unity, Peter White, a man who holds the Order of Canada, told Montreal's *La Presse* that a "sovereignty-partnership" between Canada and Quebec was a good solution to the current situation. Conservative leader Jean Charest cannot understand why the federal government is interested in proclaiming the rule of law before Quebec separatists who brazenly say· they intend to ignore it. Former Quebec Liberal leader Claude Ryan, who once said it is harmful for a francophone child to learn English before grade four, cannot understand why the prime minister would do anything to represent the interests of the "anglophone" provinces.

And these are the federalists.

We must look beyond *conditional* federalists and trust the good sense of Canadians who were smart enough to reject Charlottetown. They will be smart enough to realize the future of Canada is only in danger if we let go of it.

We must stand up not only to the separatists, but also to the members of the lamb lobby, who have validated every separatist argument. Despite what you hear from the separatists and their fellow travellers, Canada is *not* broken. Canada is *not* divided. It is Quebec that is divided between federalists on one side and separatists on the other. Federalists in Quebec love being part of this diverse, democratic nation.

Lucien Bouchard denies that Canada even has a right to be called a country. He has described this great country as a prison, while Deputy Premier Bernard Landry has said that Jean Chrétien is worse than a totalitarian dictator.

Most Quebecers are far too intelligent to swallow such drivel. But what prompts separatists like Lucien Bouchard and Bernard Landry to use words like "prison" and "totalitarian"? The answer is, they say it because they know they can get away with it. They know the federal government is too high-minded to get its hands dirty by going head-on against them.

We're so used to this being the case, that we were stunned when Jean Chrétien finally decided that even the separatists and the Quebec National Assembly are not above the law.

If the leader of any other country said that he would stand up for the rule of law, no one would pay the slightest attention. In Canada, it makes front-page news.

But, to quote Bob Dylan, "the times they are a-changin'." At some point, we have to stop talking about the perpetual threat of separatism and do something about it.

That time is now.

Turning Back the Tide

There's no need to reinvent the wheel. We can learn from the separatists, who were completely prepared for either outcome on October 30, 1995. If they had managed to steal enough votes to get a victory, they had billions of dollars in liquid cash to prop up the Canadian dollar. They had delegations prepared to travel to international financial capitals to reassure investors. They would also have been helped by the international media, whose blazing headlines on October 31 would have read, "Birth of a Nation."

In order to reassure jittery financial markets, Jean Chrétien and Lucien Bouchard would have held a joint press conference to tell the world that the situation was an internal matter and that it was still business as usual. By the time a lame duck like Daniel Johnson demanded a recount, it would have been too late.

If there had been a Yes vote last time, the separatists would have had it all. Total independence alongside a sweetheart deal with Canada to cushion the blow. Lucien Bouchard would literally have dictated the terms of Canada's surrender. And if Chrétien would have dared do anything to stand up for Canada, Bouchard would have threatened a unilateral declaration of independence. It would have been a sucker deal for Canada, but Jean Chrétien and his fellow Canadians would have been too stunned and shocked to realize that they just had their country stolen from them.

Partition would have been out of the question since the Quebec Liberals had succeeded in sweeping the issue under the carpet and prevented people from even talking about it, much less making plans for it. The millions of French Canadians who thought they were voting for a better deal would have been in for a rude awakening. But, as Jacques Parizeau said, once the lobsters were in the pot, it would have been too late to do anything. They would have found themselves outside Canada, stuck in a xenophobic French republic with a huge debt, civil unrest, and half the population in a state of complete turmoil.

That would have happened then. It will never happen now.

Canadians across this great land have finally realized that you don't appreciate what you have until you almost lose it. The prime minister has finally realized that he must stand up for the rule of law. He must defend the interests of all Canadians.

And if the separatists are offended, so be it. Twenty-eight million Canadians should be offended at a vocal minority of separatists who want to destroy this country. Canadians are fed up with separatists who believe in the right of self-determination for the people of Quebec if they vote Yes, but ignore the fact that Quebecers showed their right to self-determination on October 30, 1995. And they determined they want to stay in Canada. Canadians are fed up with hypocritical separatists who believe that 50 percent plus one is enough to break up a country, but not enough to keep it together.

What can we do? We can take a lesson from the separatists. We *too* must be prepared for either outcome the next time around.

The results of the next referendum must only be accepted by Canada if they are binding. If there is a No vote for the third time, there must be a constitutional amendment to prevent any future referendums on the breakup of Canada. France and the United States do not allow referendums on the issue of national unity, yet no one questions the fact that they are great democracies. Referendums on secession must be disallowed by law because narrow-minded, xenophobic nationalists who refuse to accept the democratic desire of Quebecers to stay in Canada must not be allowed to hold the entire country hostage whenever they feel like it.

To be properly prepared for the next time, do what the separatists do. The last time around, they passed contingency legislation in the National Assembly about what would happen in the event of a Yes vote. It's time to pass contingency legislation in the House of Commons. It only helps the separatists if Quebecers can merely guess what will happen after a Yes. If we don't spell out clearly what are the costs and consequences of separation, the separatists will paint a rosy picture of a sweetheart deal dictated to an English Canada cowering on its knees. With contingency legislation in the House of Commons, Quebecers won't have to guess what will happen in the event of a Yes vote. They will know exactly what will happen.

Sure the debate will be divisive. But as Intergovernmental Affairs Minister Stéphane Dion said, it is better to discuss all these matters in advance, and not at the last minute, two weeks before another referendum.

Canada, which is already one of the most decentralized countries in the world, continues to be weakened by power-hungry political premiers who are more interested in creating their own fiefdoms than they are in creating a more powerful and united country. It's time for our leaders to get with the program, and that means working to keep this nation strong and united. And they need ordinary citizens to spell out this program to them in no uncertain terms.

The veterans in the last war did not fight for provincial jurisdictions. They fought and they died for Canada and for freedom.

PART 2

THE PLAYERS

When it comes to the issue of breaking up the country, there are really only two viewpoints: either you want to split Quebec apart from the rest of Canada, or you want to keep the country together. That seems simple enough, right? Well, because this is Canada, it's never that simple.

Hardline separatists want Quebec to secede from Canada, whatever the cost. Strongly committed federalists are determined to preserve the country, within the rule of law. Both of these groups know exactly what they want. However, there are a number of groups who are ambivalent about Canada and what a great country it is. Each of these three ambivalent groups has its own particular line of reasoning, but they all share one thing in common: they are divorced from reality. Their ambivalence about this country plays into the hands of the separatists while it undermines those strongly committed to federalism. This is why, in spite of the No vote in the last referendum, there is the perception that the separatists are winning.

There are, then, five major groups of players within the debate over Quebec's separation from Canada:

1. Hardline Separatists
2. Conditional Federalists and Soft Nationalists

3. The "Lamb Lobby"
4. The Nihilist Left
5. Committed Federalists

Let us discuss each group in turn.

Hardline Separatists

Hardline separatists, such as those who belong to the Parti Québécois and the Bloc Québécois, want to break up Canada and create a French republic of Quebec. This is their goal, and most days they are perfectly honest and will admit this. They claim to want this for a couple of reasons.

1. Quebec is more than a province within Canada — it is a separate nation

When Lucien Bouchard said that Canada is not a real country, he said it because he feels that what we call Canada is in fact two nations, one English and one French, which never made a deal. He's lying. They did make a deal. The deal in 1867 was to form one political nation made up of English Canadians and French Canadians. And what we see today, as we approach the twenty-first century, is the peaceful coexistence of English Canadians, French Canadians, new Canadians, and native peoples, who have all worked together to build this country. This is a concept believed in and respected by twenty-eight million citizens of this country. Two million of its citizens disagree. They say there are two nations: a French nation and an English nation.

That's not the case. What is commonly referred to as English Canada is not "English" at all, in the ethnic sense, but rather is composed of immigrants from every corner of the earth. There is no English nation. People living in the rest of Canada do not think of themselves as living in the

English Nation of Canada. Only in Quebec is this idea taken seriously, and only by a minority at that.

Now, the two million people who want to believe in this concept of two nations happen to be — what a coincidence! — the same people who want to separate from Canada and turn Quebec into a French state. Why would we accept the thesis of the two million who want to break up the country, and throw out the thesis of the twenty-eight million who want to keep it together?

Hardline separatists want to turn back the clock. Lucien Bouchard's vision for Quebec is based on the nineteenth-century nationalist view of nationhood: one nation, one ethnic group. That's no longer fashionable in today's world, of course, so he won't try to promote his vision that way. He tries to promote it instead as territorial nationalism.

Once again, he's lying. There are 3.5 million Quebecers who do not want to be part of this new French nation. This is never mentioned by the sovereignists, and again, it should be said by the federalists, and that's why I'm saying it right here. *There are 3.5 million Quebecers who do not feel they are part of the Quebec nation; they feel they are part of the Canadian nation. And that's the way they want to stay.*

Is there a Quebec nation? Quebec is a province. You could say that there is a French Canadian nation, six million members of which live in Quebec, while one million live in the rest of Canada. And there are also one million people who live in Quebec who are not part of the French Canadian nation, and who do not want to be part of an independent French republic of Quebec. They already feel they are part of the nation of Canada.

2. The will of the people of Quebec is to separate from Canada

Even if they have a hard time erasing history and "proving" that Canada as it now stands is illegitimate because it never arrived at a deal with Quebec, separatists maintain that the bulk of Quebecers no longer believe that their true interests are represented in Ottawa, and thus want to control their own destiny by forming their own state.

Does it matter that "The People" have already said no to separation, not once but twice? Not in the least. The separatist version of democracy is accepting what the people have to say, provided it's what the separatists want to hear. If it isn't, they ignore it. When it comes to holding a referendum on sovereignty, the rules are that the separatists win if they get a 50-percent-plus-one vote to a trick question, to a partnership that has not been agreed on, of which there is no guarantee whatsoever.

Fifty percent plus one isn't enough to change the rules of a corporation, mind you. But even if you accept these terms — and our federal government has been stupid enough to accept them on two different occasions — the No side still won. In 1980 we had 60 percent, and in 1995 we had 50.6 percent. Both times, Canada's side won. The people have spoken.

In any election, when one side wins, the losing side says, "Well, democracy has spoken, the people have spoken; we will go along with the results." In this case, however, the losing side did not go along with it. The second it was over, they said, "We're gonna continue to hold referendums till we get a Yes vote." They said if they need three or four or five or six or seven referendums, they will hold as many referendums as it takes.

In other words, they're saying, "We will continue asking the people what they want until the people tell us what we want to hear." How's that for a lose-lose situation for Canada? And once "The People" have said Yes once, that's it for all future referendums on separation. Just as France has a law preventing all referendums on breaking itself apart, so too will an independent Quebec.

That is the twisted separatist notion of democracy.

When you add to this the fact that the chief electoral officer is appointed for life, is a good friend of the founder of separatism, and refuses to check into ballot fraud, this is about as far from democracy as you can get. It's a perversion of the word.

In short, the separatists really don't care about the "will of the people." They only care about the will of their supporters. And the only people among whom separation enjoys majority support are French Quebecers, though, even here, the people have to be tricked with false questions into supporting sovereignty. Non–French Quebecers vote consistently and overwhelmingly to stay in Canada. Why is this? Because most of them understand that they are not welcome in an independent Quebec.

The situation has become so bad in Quebec in terms of federalists not standing up for themselves that they've put up with language laws that have turned them into second-class citizens. There is Bill 86, for instance, which says that people are permitted to post English signs, provided they are half the number of French signs in a given establishment, or that they are half the size. Now, this is an insult and a humiliation to anglophones, but until recently most of them have accepted this as a *reasonable* compromise, just to show how much they enjoy living in Quebec. They *love* the French fact, so much so that they are willing to have their language literally *belittled* in favour of French.

Bill 86 shows that anglophones have bent over backwards, yet for language hardliners it's not enough. They want to erase the public face of English from the province. They don't want to see *any* English. Period. They see anything else as caving in. Federalists and sovereignist hardliners are so far apart that separatists see Lucien Bouchard's Centaur Theatre address, where the premier reportedly "stretched out his hand to anglophones," as some sort of failed attempt at conciliation. This is totally preposterous for several reasons.

First of all, there was nothing in his hand. He said that when someone requires medical attention, they don't need a language test. Meanwhile, his government closes anglophone hospitals. Those that are left open have crowded emergency wards, whereas the francophone hospitals don't suffer nearly as much. On sovereignty, he offered nothing. In terms of language, what was the concession he gave the anglophone community? Reviving the language police and giving them an operating budget of $5 million to have the right to come into your office and search through your files.

In Iraq? No. In Quebec.

This is an indication of just how far things have gone.

When members of the anglophone community decided not to put up with this attempt to totally ignore their presence, they were within their legal rights. The Quebec Political Action Committee, in conjunction with an alliance of grassroots organizations in Quebec, got together and threatened to boycott chain stores in the English-speaking areas of Montreal that weren't carrying at least *some* English signs. Yet when anglophones say they're going to spend their money where they're treated with a modicum of respect, separatist hardliners such as *Gazette* columnist Ed Bantey refer to this as "economic blackmail."

(When federalists in Quebec talk about the reality that you can't just hijack 3.5 million people from one jurisdiction to another against their will, Bantey and his fellow travellers call this "the threat of partition." The partition of Canada is never mentioned.)

Bantey feels that Lucien Bouchard is too much of a nice guy when it comes to the English-speaking community. In his August 4, 1996, column on the proposed boycott, he said that "this was a case of the tail endeavoring to wag the dog." To separatist hardliners, anglo "drum beaters" are the "tail" wagging Quebec. In other words, anglophones are running Quebec.

This is too hysterical for words.

The truth of the matter is that the metaphor of the tail wagging the dog does make a lot of sense. It is *Quebec* that tells *Canada* what to do, and sets all the rules while the rest of Canada nods like a dog and does what it is told.

Bantey said, "Bouchard's obsession with consensus and reconciliation has come to nothing." I don't see any consensus and I don't see any reconciliation that Bouchard has presented, but Ed Bantey does. The truth is, *there is no room for consensus. There is no room for reconciliation.* You either have one country or you have two countries. The separatist movement wants to break this country apart and create a separate ethnocentric state. Period. That's not an opinion; that's a fact. And most of them will be honest enough to tell you this on most occasions.

The other option is that you work to keep this country together, because the vast majority — twenty-eight million people — are quite satisfied with it, thank you very much.

Myth: The French Language Needs Special Protection — More than Canada Is Currently Offering It

One of the key myths the separatists use to get the people of Quebec mad or frightened enough to vote for their option is the idea that the French language is on the verge of dying in Quebec, all due to the threat of bilingualism. Of course, this is the biggest lie there is. Is Italian in danger of dying in Quebec? Is German in danger of dying in Quebec? How come German people still speak German? They're surrounded by a sea of non-Germans. Italians are surrounded by a sea of non-Italians, yet they continue to teach their children the Italian language and culture. Do you know why so many young Italians in their twenties and thirties speak fluent Italian? Because they *want* to. And these are languages that don't even benefit from having their status officially enshrined in the Canadian Constitution.

Language hardliners such as Gilles Rhéaume, of the Mouvement Souvérainiste du Québec, are not above using the vilest rhetoric to drum up support for their cause. On an open-line radio show, Rhéaume went beyond describing Canada as a prison; he called it a "cemetery" for French Canadians. Some cemetery! Yet, even if we went along with this mindless drivel, a separate Quebec which outlawed English, closed down English radio and television stations, blocked signals, and banned American movies would certainly not be more effective in protecting the French language. What would the language hardliners do if they overheard a bunch of kids talking English on the street corner? Forbid them from speaking English on the corner? English is not going to go away, regardless of whether or not Quebec separates. The only way the French language and culture is going to be protected is if people protect it themselves.

Separatists have succeeded in convincing many people that an independent Quebec will be better able to protect the French language and culture. Well, I don't doubt that they'd go even further in passing one repressive language law after another against the English-speaking minority. But in terms of actual protection, the truth of the matter is that *Canada* has done the most to protect the French language, through its policy of official bilingualism. And Canadians have not only come to accept this policy, they have embraced it. People in the rest of Canada are lining up for French immersion courses. These are anglophones who don't *need* to know French, yet they *want* to learn it.

If Quebec ever were to separate and become a completely independent French country, it would become Louisiana

II within a generation. Outside of the Canadian confederation, Quebec would become a tiny pocket of French surrounded by an English-speaking North America. The only way French Quebecers could deal with anybody who didn't come from their own country would be to learn English. No government could stop the attraction for English among its citizens — especially its youth — and within a generation or two the French language here would disappear, or become merely quaint.

How does Canada protect the French language, you ask? Where would I get such a notion? Well, I can give you *billions* of reasons, literally. Billions of dollars that Canadian taxpayers have spent on official bilingualism.

Official bilingualism means ensuring, on one hand, that French shares equal prominence with English in every federally funded institution across Canada, from post offices to airports — even in areas where no one speaks a word of French — and then, on the other hand, turning to Quebec and saying it's okay for the National Assembly to make French the only official language in Quebec. *No problem.* Bill 101 passes, and Trudeau backs off, saying he's not going to do anything about it. Bill 178 passes, and the Mulroney government says it's not going to do anything about it. Lucien Bouchard is the federal government's minister in charge of official languages when Bill 178 is passed.

Canada has spent a fortune on the French language. It has made French and English its official languages across the country, from coast to coast. French Canadians run the government. The parliament is run bilingually. A unilingual French Canadian who didn't speak a word of English until he was an adult — Jean Chrétien — went on to become the prime minister of this country.

This country has done plenty to promote French. And it has let Quebec pass one racist law after another against

Canadian citizens living here. In 1988, former premier Robert Bourassa stood up, on Canadian soil, in the National Assembly and said that he had suspended fundamental human liberties in order to protect the French language. The government in Ottawa did nothing about it. That is how far the Canadian government has gone to protect the French language.

All of this is the so-called "repressive federalism" that's a crucial part of the separatist mythology. That's how repressive it is. It allows Quebec to pass one racist law after another, which its *own courts* deem racist.

The fraudulent notion that the French language is in danger is the excuse that successive Quebec governments have been using to create two classes of citizens in Quebec, and once in a while one of their leaders has the decency to tell the truth about it. When Jacques Parizeau blamed the referendum loss on the ethnics and money, he made a comment that showed the true picture of separatism, which is ethnic nationalism, pure and simple. And let me tell you: it is not enough to *speak* French; you have to *be* French. Anybody who questions that can just look at a roster of who's employed by the Quebec civil service. When was the last time Quebec had an English premier? Never mind the notion of ever having one, the mere *thought* of it is out of the question. And we're not supposed to pay attention to this. It's impolite to mention it.

Well, I think it's very important to bring it up.

The prime minister of Canada is almost always from Quebec. And he can't only be elected in one province; he has to be elected by the rest of Canada, too. Now, you'd think this would send a positive message to Quebecers, but is it accepted as such? No, nothing is ever accepted as a positive message here, because the mythology has to be maintained that English Canada is the oppressor, and that French Canadians are an oppressed minority — even though trying to argue this would get you laughed out of any international forum.

Ethnic Nationalism: Us versus Them

There are several misconceptions surrounding Jacques Parizeau's comments on referendum night when he blamed the result on "money" and "the ethnic vote." Many people forget that not only did he say the words, he practically spat them out. They also forget that he spoke of "revenge," repeating the word several times.

Apologists have said that Parizeau didn't really mean it. The separatists, many now claim, didn't agree with what he said, and were appalled by the comments.

Oh, really?

First of all, they applauded his remarks. They did not walk out of the hall when he made them. Secondly, Parizeau did not apologize for his remarks then, and he has not apologized since. And for a very good reason. With Jacques Parizeau, what you see is what you get. He meant what he said.

Hardline separatists think it's a waste of time making any concessions to anglophones, because they will never support sovereignty. Those hardliners are absolutely right. Anglophones are consistently being deprived of their rights even though Quebec is still part of Canada. English signs have to be half the size or half the number of French signs in Quebec, and even that is seen as too great a concession. Hardliners have no shame in saying that the only way to protect the French language and culture is to obliterate the English language from public view. So, why would self-respecting anglophones possibly want to vote to make themselves second-class citizens of a floundering new country, where they would be made into scapegoats if anything went wrong in the separatist paradise of an independent Quebec.

Parti Québécois MNA Monique Simard has said that reducing the project of a sovereign Quebec to racism is an insult. Well, if the shoe fits, wear it. It is the comments of separatists like former premier Jacques Parizeau and Deputy Premier Bernard Landry that are insulting.

Bernard Landry is a man given to insulting ethnic hotel clerks and blaming them for the referendum loss. This is a man who is so out of touch with reality that he said the overabundance of For Sale and For Rent signs throughout Montreal is proof that the economy is improving. Landry has such a low regard for the intelligence of Quebecers that he actually expects them to believe such nonsense.

It must be granted, however, that the PQ does indeed have a sense of humour. Monique Simard managed, with a straight face, to say that the PQ executive would urge the party to adopt an "action plan" with measures specifically aimed at minorities. We can just imagine. So far, one of the warmhearted measures aimed at minorities has been the reinstatement of the tongue troopers — a.k.a. the language police — who will have the right to search business establishments to ensure that they are conducting their business with enough French to suit the wishes of the collectivity.

The PQ is pursuing this attempt to further interfere with business, as if business in Quebec didn't have enough problems, with the chronic economic uncertainty brought about by the perpetual threat of separation. (In Montreal, for instance, it has been reported that for every single homebuyer, there are twenty-one houses for sale on the market.)

While most PQ hardliners thrill at the idea of seeking revenge by making it more difficult for anglophones to live in Quebec, the vast majority of Quebecers are ashamed and embarrassed at what such measures do to the reputation of Quebec in the rest of Canada and around the world.

Does the PQ have any serious intention of adopting an action plan for minorities? Of course not. If it did, it might consider hiring anglophones in the Quebec civil service, which is almost exclusively white and *pure laine* francophone. If the PQ were serious about doing something for the anglophones in Quebec, it might consider removing racist language laws or undoing some of the ridiculous sign laws. The PQ might start respecting democracy and realize that No means No.

Will the PQ do any of this? Sure they will. And Santa Claus lives in a time share at the North Pole.

Every now and then, though, the PQ does make some noise about extending the warm hand of friendship to anglophones. I told you they had a sense of humour. For example, a headline on the front page of the *Gazette* on May 28, 1996, read, "Bouchard Shows Concern Over Anglos' Plans." According to the article, the premier said that a survey revealing that six out of ten English-speaking Quebecers say they'll leave the province if it separates "has to be given some attention."

Anyone who really believes that Lucien Bouchard is seriously concerned about anglophones leaving Quebec is dreaming in technicolour. Why on earth would he be concerned about anglophones? Anglophones don't vote for Lucien Bouchard. Anglophones don't vote for separation. The more anglophones leave, the less need to steal their votes. The less need to steal votes, the fewer obstacles for the separatists as they attempt the largest land grab in North American history.

If Lucien Bouchard were genuinely concerned about the anglophone exodus, he would do something about it.

He has done nothing about it.

Lucien Bouchard said that if Montreal were to become

bilingual, it would be the end of the French language in Quebec. That, of course, is the usual patent PQ nonsense. But it is an integral part of the paranoid nationalist mythology. The reality is that if Montreal were to become bilingual, that still would not prevent the people in Lac-St-Jean from remaining as unilingual and insular as ever. They could still pretend to themselves that they are the only people in the world who really matter.

The separatist hardliners have a short leash on Lucien Bouchard. They will do everything they can to ensure that Montreal never becomes a bilingual city, and they don't care if they have to kill the city in the process. Separatist hardliners want to erase any public trace of the English language. While the separatists are seeking revenge for what happened centuries ago on the Plains of Abraham, the members of the anglophone "lamb lobby" are trying to build bridges.

The anglophone community has been building bridges for thirty years. It has not worked. It has made matters worse and worse. The more concessions they made, the more they learned how to speak French, the more bridges they built, the more their rights were taken away.

I am not worried about Lucien Bouchard. I know what he wants. The *raison d'être* of Lucien Bouchard and the *raison d'être* of the Parti Québécois is the breakup of Canada and the independence of Quebec by any means and at any cost.

What *does* worry me is the fact that the hardline separatists are bolstered by a group of "soft" nationalists who are as easily swayed by rhetoric as they are by the latest opinion polls. They say they want more power for Quebec, if possible within Canadian confederation, but if not, they are willing to flirt with outright separation. This flirtation is dangerous, though, because the rest of Canada is ready, willing, and able to call their bluff. They are prepared to say,

"No new deal. Canada will remain as it is, with equal rights for all of its citizens. Take it or leave it."

The soft nationalists are really pawns to the separatist hardliners. For, in fact, their obsession with "more powers for Quebec" cannot be satisfied without separation being the inevitable consequence.

Conditional Federalists and Soft Nationalists

During the last referendum, a substantial portion of the Yes vote came from Quebecers who cannot be called diehard separatists. These "soft" nationalists are under the impression that, somehow, in spite of all evidence to the contrary, Canada is holding Quebec back from achieving its full potential. Many of them are still nursing resentments that Canada has refused to alter its Constitution to recognize Quebec as a "distinct society."

Their federalism is conditional on Canada allowing Quebec to, in essence, act like a nation unto itself in all matters concerning language, culture, and even commerce. Unless Canada goes along with remaking itself in order to comply with these demands, they are entirely prepared to take the short step over the line into the separatist camp.

And these are not radicals, by the way. Far from it. These are people who have bought into the line of reasoning espoused by none other than the Quebec Liberal Party — the party that allegedly represents those *opposed* to separation.

Robert Bourassa, Daniel Johnson, and the Quebec Liberal Party

Are the Quebec Liberals part of the solution? No, they are part of the problem.

As far as Daniel Johnson is concerned, being premier of Quebec is basically a family business. His father, who was head of the Union Nationale, was premier of Quebec, and coined the phrase "Equality or Independence." Daniel Johnson, *père*, was elected premier with fewer votes than the Liberal Party, but thanks to the way the ridings were distributed he became premier nonetheless. When this was pointed out to him, he cheerfully observed that a majority of francophones had voted for him, and that was all that really counted.

Daniel Johnson's brother, Pierre-Marc Johnson, who was the head of the Parti Québécois, was also a premier of Quebec. Naturally, Daniel Johnson also had to become premier, which he did as leader of the Quebec Liberal Party — an organization that has done as much to undermine the federation as the Parti Québécois ever did. Johnson took over the nationalist Quebec Liberal Party from Robert Bourassa, who, along with Brian Mulroney, helped to revive and reawaken separatist sentiment when it was dead in the water in the early 1980s.

Ever the staunch nationalist, Bourassa flirted with separation on many occasions, but would usually realize where Quebec's bread was really buttered. He was the grand master of the good cop-bad cop routine. He would tell Canada, "Hand over whatever I want or the *really bad separatists* will get in." And the routine worked splendidly for many years, resulting in Quebec making billions of dollars at the expense of the rest of Canada, all the while complaining that it was never enough, and, of course, humiliating.

Bourassa reneged on his promise to allow bilingual signs, even though he won the premiership in 1985 with a commanding 99 seats in the 122-seat National Assembly. He stood up in the National Assembly to proudly assert that he had suspended fundamental liberties to protect the

French language. He was the one who gave us Bill 150, allowing the province of Quebec to hold its own referendum on sovereignty. He created the concept of a unilateral declaration of independence, which even former PQ premier René Lévesque refused to accept on grounds that it was undemocratic.

Robert Bourassa is the man who flew out West to testify against education rights for francophones outside Quebec, because he was worried that he might have to extend the same considerations to anglophones inside Quebec. Bourassa was the one who suggested to Lucien Bouchard that he form the Bloc Québécois. During his entire career, he never ceased attacking and undermining Canada. Nonetheless, his ability at fence-straddling was so impressive that he managed to convince many people he was actually a *federalist*.

Bourassa is the man who told Quebec nationalists who were vehemently opposed to the Meech Lake Accord not to worry, since it would only be the consolation prize. And for those of you who wax nostalgic about Meech and wonder if the separatist movement would have been defused if only Meech had been ratified, remember the words of the great philosopher Barbara Streisand, who once sang, "Can it be that it was all so simple then — or has time rewritten every line?"

It has indeed.

The fact is, Meech would have settled nothing, with the possible exception that the distinct society clause would have enabled Quebec governments to further discriminate against non-francophones without the embarrassment of having to invoke the notwithstanding clause every time they wanted to remove another fundamental right. Those in the rest of Canada, who may have thought that Meech would settle everything, would have been rudely awakened by a brand new set of demands from the Quebec Liberal Party, which were eventually published in the Allaire Report. The basic tenet of the Allaire Report was an insult to the intelligence of the rest of Canada, calling on the federal government to give Quebec practically all the powers of a separate country, or else Quebec would threaten to *become* a separate country.

It is amazing that British Columbia, which throughout its history has been treated like garbage by Ottawa, still hasn't figured out how you get the federal government to give you what you want. Threaten to separate, and next time you need any more power and/or money, threaten to separate again. This has worked extremely well for Quebec for decades. It is such an obvious tactic that Lucien Bouchard was barely out of school when he wrote an essay on how threatening to separate was the best way to extract concessions from the rest of Canada.

The Allaire Report outlined Quebec's twenty-two constitutional demands. Quebec would take over every jurisdiction with the exception of — get this — currency, the common debt, and equalization payments. In essence, Ottawa would still be allowed to send money to Quebec, and, what the hell, it could still be in charge of defence and postage stamps.

Again, I must reiterate, I am not making this up.

Basically, this was separation with transfer payments. Junior would promise not to leave the house, provided that he was allowed to run the family business, and was given the family car, all the while magnanimously allowing Dad to continue paying his allowance.

And, by the way, this was the handiwork of the Quebec Liberal Party. When Jean Allaire could not get his way with his Christmas wish list, he formed his own party, the Parti Action Démocratique, which was then led by Mario Dumont, who (surprise, surprise) said that he would vote Yes in last October's referendum, even though he did not consider himself a separatist!

When it comes to finding even a germ of federalism anywhere in Quebec politics, it is very hard to tell the players without a program. If there were such a program, Daniel Johnson, *fils*, would be listed under the federalists. As a matter of fact, many pundits have suggested that Daniel Johnson is the most federalist leader the Quebec Liberal Party has ever had.

No wonder we are in such trouble.

When he first became leader of the Liberal Party, Johnson said that he was a Canadian first and foremost. He learned the error of his ways in less than twenty-four hours. He recanted immediately, saying that that was not what he really meant to say and that he probably wasn't feeling well when he said it — if he did say it, which he might not have under the circumstances.

During the election campaign in 1994, he could have told the electorate, "Vote for me, and the borders of Quebec will always remain intact. Vote for Jacques Parizeau, and you don't know what will happen." He *could* have said that, but he chose not to say it. When asked if a 50-percent-plus-one vote to a trick question is all that is needed to break up a country like Canada, his response was, "A win is a win."

Daniel Johnson's flag is in mint condition. Before the referendum, he could barely bring himself to say the word "Canada." He would always be talking about the "Canadian Union" or the "Canadian Economic Space." Is Canada good enough for Daniel Johnson? Of course not. Quebec must first be recognized in the Constitution as a distinct society.

And what if it isn't? Does this mean that Daniel Johnson will become a separatist and work to break up Canada? Lucien Bouchard has obviously given that some thought. In the last few days before the referendum, Bouchard said that after the vote there would be no federalists or separatists — only Quebecers who would join him in getting the best possible deal out of the rest of Canada.

True enough, at least for Daniel Johnson. He would certainly stay, and he wouldn't exactly be a supporter of partition either. As far as Daniel Johnson is concerned, the borders of Quebec are sacred. What a pity he doesn't feel nearly the same fervour about protecting the borders of Canada.

Daniel Johnson isn't overly concerned with the question of whether or not Quebec has the right to self-determination. Nor is he upset about the possibility of a unilateral declaration of independence. How could he be upset? It was his party that came up with the concept in the first place!

Does Daniel Johnson have a solution to the national unity problem? Sure he does. Just vote for him and the Quebec Liberal Party, enshrine distinct society status in the Constitution, give Quebec the veto, and we will all live happily ever after.

These "solutions," of course, are completely ridiculous. First of all, the way the ridings are set up in Quebec, the hinterland rules the roost, so the chance of the Daniel Johnson Liberals winning more seats than the ruling Parti Québécois are nil. Daniel Johnson could not beat Lucien Bouchard at solitaire. And as for distinct society, it's dead and buried, but no one has apparently bothered to tell Johnson, who clings to this hopeless concept which has been rejected at Meech and during the national referendum on the Charlottetown Accord. The concept is more hated now than it ever was, and that's saying something. The separatists have effectively dismissed it as too little, too late.

The members of the Bloc Québécois proudly voted against it in the House of Commons. The government of Quebec has indicated clearly that it is not interested in the concept. So why should the rest of Canada turn itself into a pretzel and sell out the minorities in Quebec in exchange for giving Quebec something it absolutely and resolutely does not want?

Conditional Federalists

There are varying types and degrees of conditional federalists. Some are virtually indistinguishable from the soft nationalists. These are federalists who believe in Canada . . . sort of. Yes, they believe in Canada *if* it fixes itself, but not as it is. "Yes," they say, "I'll believe in Canada if you give me distinct society."

People have called to tell me they used to be federalists, but then they listened to my talk show and became very upset, so they decided to become sovereignists. These are very conditional federalists, indeed. Anything can throw them off. Because of a comment they don't like on a talk show, they're willing to go from building and believing in a country to breaking it up. And I imagine that, with these people, a headache could have the same effect. The day before, when they felt good, they were pro-Canada; today, they've woken up with a migraine, so they figure, "Oh, the hell with it. Break up Canada." So now they're separatists.

These aren't genuine federalists to begin with, of course, but the reason they continue to think it's all right to flirt with separation is that another type of conditional federalist, in the name of placating the soft nationalists, does everything to help the separatists' cause. Some of these hysterics over the years have included people like Robert Bourassa and Brian Mulroney, who said that if Meech Lake didn't go through, it would be the end of Canada. Even Stéphane Dion, who has in the past shown himself to be a strong, principled federalist, has contributed to the separatist cause by saying, "If we don't get distinct society, Canada's finished."

What better quote could a separatist want than that? A year or two down the road, just before the next referendum, when Quebec still doesn't have distinct society, all the separatists would have to do is just repeat an old Stéphane Dion quote, an old Robert Bourassa quote, an old Brian Mulroney quote — any of them. And they would say to the soft nationalists, "Listen, these guys are federalists. They're on *your* side. *They* say that if there's no distinct society, Canada's finished. *We're agreeing* with them. So, now that Canada is finished, let's discuss the terms."

That's why these conditional federalists are so dangerous. They're running around yelling that the sky is falling, when, in fact, Canada is fine and has been doing very well for 130 years without the concept of distinct society.

A lot of these same people were the ones who said that if only Meech would go through, everything would be fine. Who benefited from these kinds of scare tactics? The hard-line separatists, that's who. The sovereignists pretend to be upset at all the people who destroyed Meech, but they themselves didn't want Meech in the first place! They said it was a humiliation to Quebec. Everything, of course, is a humiliation to Quebec, except for out-and-out sovereignty.

The separatists can't do it alone. These conditional federalists are basically playing on the sovereignist side of the battlefield. They're saying, "The sovereignists are right, in the sense that Canada's really not very good as it is. *They're* going too far, because they want to break it up. *We say*, 'Yes, we agree that the current situation is bad, but we can fix it within Canada.' " They're basically buying into the argument that there's something wrong, instead of promoting the reality that there isn't anything substantially wrong with Canada. There's less wrong with Canada than with any other nation. It's already one of the most decentralized countries, if not *the* most decentralized country, in the entire world, as it is. And francophones thrive in it. Millions of them are very attached to Canada. Millions of others are not, but this is not a reason to twist it and contort it into any shape or form to placate those who will not be placated.

Soft Nationalists

The soft nationalist is the person who is worshipped in Canada. Everything done in the Canadian political spectrum is done for this one constituency. The separatists woo them because they want to increase the Yes vote. The federalists woo them because they want to add them to the No tally. The federal government is afraid that if it does anything to stand up for Canada, the soft nationalists will be alienated. So, the entire country listens to and worships and is at the beck and call of the soft nationalists.

We are told that the soft nationalists would like Quebec to separate, but if we tempt them with an offer, they'll stay. They're ready to vote to break up the country or to not break it up, and the reason they feel this way is that, as far as the federal government is concerned, the difference between those two options is no big deal. What does it matter which way you vote in a referendum on Quebec sovereignty? The separatists are saying, "Listen, you get a better deal if you vote Yes. You get more from the federal government. We get independence, we get our own way, we get to spend our own money." They have an endless list of reasons as to why you should vote Yes. And they say that if you vote No, you're just voting for the status quo.

The response from the federal government is — nothing. A resounding silence. They've been lying to the public and misleading Quebecers about the true consequences of separation. Why? Because they don't want to alienate the soft nationalists. This strategy is counterproductive, because, let me tell you, the soft nationalists aren't that committed to

55

breaking up Canada. And when they find out that separation involves a huge social cost, including the loss of territory, when they find out that their citizenship is in danger, when they find out that their taxes will double or triple in order to pay for an independent Quebec, they'll rethink their position.

But they can't find out this information in an isolated speech, or in this book. That's not enough. That doesn't have the imprimatur, the power of something that has *real meaning*. It has to come from the prime minister's office. It has to come from the federal government, in charge of all thirty million Canadian citizens, and in charge of protecting the twenty-eight million people who don't want to break up this country. The federal government has to say to the nationalists in Quebec, "We're looking out for the interests of these people. If you leave, these are the terms, and these are what will have to be discussed."

And the federalists in Ottawa can't just say this off the cuff in a rare speech somewhere outside of Quebec, or in a scrum when they're speaking to reporters. They have to say it with power and impact. They have to pass contingency legislation in the House of Commons. Have the bitter, acrimonious debate between the federalists and the separatists, and then move on to passing clear legislation. When Quebecers see this, many of them will say, "Wait a minute. This is just the *debate*. We're just talking about it *in theory*, and look at all the uncertainty it's causing."

Last time, we were afraid to address what would happen in the event of a Yes vote, because doing so would have meant we were contemplating the possibility that a Yes vote could happen. *Well, let's get over that right now.* Let the cat out of the bag! Certainly, a Yes vote can indeed happen, and in all likelihood it will happen, unless the federal government does something about clearly explaining to Quebecers what the consequences will be.

Thus far, they've been told separation is a fabulous deal and they've been given a list of advantages. Where's the downside? Are the separatists going to explain the downside to them? Of course not. No salesman explains what's wrong with his product. It's up to the other salesmen to do that. And what they present has to carry the weight of law. *These are the laws, and we expect them to be obeyed. The day after a Yes vote, the laws of Canada will still apply. A unilateral declaration of independence is out of the question, and if you declare one, we will not recognize it.*

What can you, reader, do to help? Talk to your local MP, and say, "I'm a federalist, I love this country. What are you doing to protect my rights?" And if he or she tells you, "Well, I'm pushing distinct society," that's when you've got to scream blue murder. That's going to accomplish nothing but make it that much easier for the separatists to win.

Last time, no downside was presented; next time, it's got to be presented clearly. We have to put all the facts on the table, no matter who's offended. The federal government hasn't even been willing to bring up the issue of which laws will apply in the event of a Yes vote — the laws of Canada or the laws of Quebec. This is critical. In order to maintain political authority over a given territory, one side will have to achieve effective control over that territory. If there are competing jurisdictions, competing governments trying to apply their own laws in the same regions, we need to know who will apply legitimate, effective control — Canada or Quebec.

Both Jean Chrétien and Stéphane Dion have already gone on record saying that Canada will not use force in order to keep Quebecers in Canada against their will. The same reassurance has not been forthcoming from the separatist government of Lucien Bouchard. As a matter of fact, the separatists have said that anybody who disobeys the law in an independent Quebec will be treated like a criminal. So they are prepared to use force. But they need to understand that they cannot simply make up the law as they go along.

The Clear Choice

The choice is as follows: either you work to keep Canada together, or you help to break it apart. Those are the only two options. Now, conditional federalists would like to pretend — and those include the Progressive Conservative party — that we should muddy the waters by putting in a third option, one which says, *No, don't keep Canada the way it is now. No, don't separate. Just completely reconfigure Canada and that'll be the solution.* We've tried that and it doesn't work. Muddying the waters, confusion — that has to be thrown out once and for all. It already has been, but the usual conditional federalists keep resurfacing to confuse it even further.

Progressive Conservative leader Jean Charest has mentioned the prospect of "shared sovereignty"; Peter White, head of the Council for Canadian Unity, has floated the notion that "sovereignty partnership" might be the way to go. These ideas just confuse the issue. They are not possibilities. The possibilities are Canada as one country, one nation, where English Canadians, French Canadians, new Canadians, and native peoples coexist peacefully, or two separate countries. Let's get that clear. Let's get rid of all the other options and leave only those two on the table — that's how we should make our own choice.

If Daniel Johnson is still the leader of the Liberal Party by the time you read this book, he won't be listening to any of this advice. He will still be selling the stale notion of distinct society. All that matters for Johnson is getting more powers for Quebec. And if Canada has to collapse under the weight of these impossible demands, so be it.

By the way, Daniel Johnson is not the only prominent Quebecer whose federalism is softer than Delsey tissue. In *Visions of Canada*, a 1991 book of interviews compiled by Knowlton Nash, the late Jeanne Sauvé, former governor general of Canada, was asked what she would do if Quebec separated from Canada.

"I would stay in Quebec," she replied. "This is my home, and I would live with it."

When Nash countered by responding, "You would find it pretty uncomfortable, from what you are saying," Sauvé said, "I don't think so. I am close to a lot of prominent separatists; they were my former friends and they remain friends."

That's a large part of the problem. The leaders of this country still don't get it. They just don't seem to understand that the separatists are not simply fun-loving folk, brimming with *joie de vivre*. Their goal is the destruction of this great country against the wishes of 90 percent of its population. Can you imagine any other country where a federalist leader — the representative of the Queen, no less! — would see nothing wrong with saying that she is very close to a lot of prominent people whose goal it is to break up her country? Do you think that French leader Jacques Chirac considers Basque separatists among his close circle of friends?

The Lamb Lobby

Throughout Canada, the political and media elite play up to the soft nationalists by granting credence to their complaints that Canada is not doing enough for Quebec. Because of their sheep-like acceptance of separatist mythology, *Gazette* columnist William Johnson has called these passive anglo federalists within Quebec the "lamb lobby."

Their fatal flaw is their refusal to even acknowledge all that Canada has done for Quebec and for the French fact in North America.

Federalism has been losing steadily in Quebec not because there is a legitimate reason for sovereignty; it's been losing ground steadily because members of the lamb lobby have been constantly undermining the federation by buying into the separatist argument and making it seem credible. That is why there is support for sovereignty. Not because of any genuine oppression.

We still hear about the mythical fat lady at Eaton's who, during the early 1960s, we're told, didn't speak French to her customers. That is not reason enough in 1996 to break up a great country. (It should be noted that this lady must have been one busy saleswoman. After all, millions of separatists claim to have done business with her.) But whether she was real or mythical does not even matter. That fat lady today couldn't get a job in Montreal if her life depended on it. The fat lady has obviously moved to Ontario, because today, if she doesn't speak perfect French, she can't get a job at Eaton's. Whoops, I mean Eaton.

Lambs in Canada

I've said it before and I'll say it again: last October's referendum was won for the No side not because of most Canadian politicians, but in spite of them.

In a debate held in Ontario between former prime minister Joe Clark and Lucien Bouchard, Bouchard pointed out that Clark had gone along with the patriation of the Constitution. Bouchard then asked him if he would apologize for this. Joe Clark said yes, and he apologized for it! He apologized for bringing the Constitution back from England to Canada, with the approval of most Canadians, and with the approval of most Quebecers, according to the polls, but without the approval of the separatist government.

Now, why would the separatist government want to sign the Canadian Constitution? They're a separatist government! But does that mean the people of Quebec didn't want it? Of course not.

If you're looking for a clue as to where politicians such as Joe Clark get their absurd notions, look no further than University of Ottawa political science professor John Trent, who is president of an organization called Dialogue Canada. In August 1996, Professor Trent was a guest on my show, discussing the national unity question. For the professor, the problem is not in Quebec but in the rest of Canada.

I found this quite fascinating. I thought the rest of Canada *had* its act together, realized that it was the greatest country in the world, and wanted to stay together. Period. I thought the problem was in Quebec, where the population was divided right down the middle. In the last referendum, half the people voted to stay in Canada, while the other half voted to break up Canada or for some imagined partnership.

The professor, on the other hand, believes that the problem was that the rest of Canada had not bothered to put an offer on the table. But why would the rest of Canada bother to put anything on the table when Lucien Bouchard, during the press conference at which he said he would assume the PQ leadership, stated in no uncertain terms that he didn't want to hear any offers. A reporter asked him, "Mr. Bouchard, is there anything at all that the federal government could put on the table for you to consider?" His response was very simple, clear, and concise: "No," he said. "I'm a sovereignist."

When I mentioned this to Professor Trent, he suggested

that Bouchard was just posturing. And the basic conclusion the professor came to was that Lucien Bouchard is "a sovereignist if necessary, but not necessarily a sovereignist." So, here was a federalist defending the viewpoint of someone he thinks can be bought. You don't get any better blackmail and extortion than that. *Give me what I want, or I'll break up your country.*

I confronted Professor Trent as follows: Even if the rest of Canada were willing to contort itself into a pretzel, what good would it do? Would Lucien Bouchard then be able to say to the other separatists, "You know what guys? I spoke to the other premiers in the rest of Canada, and they said they're willing to make a fabulous deal, so let's call off our lifetime goal. Forget about having our own French country, let's stay in Canada. What a great country"? He couldn't do that to his party, I said, so it's preposterous to even try to appease him. "Yes," Professor Trent responded. "It would be difficult."

Professor Trent also weighed in against the intransigence, not of Quebec separatists, but of the rest of Canada! A free and democratic country where there are no sign laws forbidding the French language from public view; where people are not forced to attend certain schools against their will. *This* is who to blame for the current situation.

Myth: By Failing To Do All We Could for Quebec Earlier, We've Helped Sow the Seeds of Nationalism in the Province

There seems to be this notion that it was Canada's stubbornness, intransigence, and unwillingness to do whatever it takes to get Quebec into the Canadian Constitution that led to the resurgence of the independence movement. Yet the only way you could arrive at this conclusion is if you weren't watching carefully as events were unfolding.

Independence was dead in the water — down to 20 or 25 percent support — until the man who bears the brunt of the responsibility for the current situation, Brian Mulroney, got together with separatists across Quebec, and with PQ organizers in order to get elected. He allowed Lucien Bouchard to write his speeches, such as the one he delivered in Sept-Iles, in which the prime minister of Canada repeated the separatist lie that Quebec had been humiliated when the Constitution was patriated in 1982.

Now, when that lie is being told to you, not by separatists, but by the prime minister of Canada, when nationalists in Quebec hear the prime minister of Canada saying that they've been humiliated, let me tell you, a decade of that really helps to build mythology, and that is what Brian Mulroney did. He resuscitated Quebec separatism. For his own purposes, he brought separatism back to life. He thought he could diffuse it later, and he didn't care if he wrecked Canada in the process. He didn't want his predecessor Pierre Trudeau to get the credit for patriating the Constitution. He wanted to accomplish what Trudeau couldn't.

He "rolled the dice." What did he care if Canada lost. He admitted as much. He rolled the dice and we all lost.

And now, we're stuck with people such as John Trent and Joe Clark repeating the same myth that Canada still is not worthy of having Quebec in the Constitution.

The final question I asked Professor Trent was, "Would you agree that Lucien Bouchard is correct in all his criticisms of Canada?"

And his response was, "You're damned right he is."

So Lucien Bouchard's complaints that Canada is not a real country, that Quebec has no place in Canada, that Canada has mishandled and mistreated Quebecers, are all right on with Professor John Trent of the University of

Ottawa. He's head of a group called Dialogue Canada, whose mission is to try to convince the rest of Canada to give in more, to appease further. If I were a proud French Quebecer who listened to this interview and I was thinking of voting for Canada, I'd say to myself, "You know, until now I've listened to the federalist argument and I really like this country, but boy, if an anglophone professor at the University of Ottawa thinks Lucien Bouchard is right, who am I to disagree? Why shouldn't I vote Yes the next time?"

People like John Trent are far more dangerous to this country than separatists, because we see the separatists for what they are — a group of people who want to create an ethnocentric French state where the interests of one ethnic group come before the interests of everyone else. But, for Professor Trent, hidden away in the groves of academe, tucked away in the ivory tower, totally unaware of how anglophones in Quebec are treated as second-class citizens and live under a government that threatens to take away their rights if they so much as ask for them, the problem is Canada's unwillingness to give Quebec more powers.

People like Professor Trent are not part of the solution; they are part of the problem. They constitute a tiny minority who still think that French Canadians are not treated well within Canada in 1996. Not only are they living in the past, they're suffering from the Stockholm Syndrome: they've been hijacked so long by this argument that they're beginning to believe the hijackers.

They're so out of step that they don't recognize that fewer and fewer *separatists* even believe that they're oppressed. Even the Union des Artistes — a staunchly nationalist union of francophones in the media and in show business — has realized that Quebecers have become hugely successful at whatever they try to do. And they've succeeded within the context of Canada as it is today, without erasing every public trace of English, without distinct society status, without separation, without $5 million being spent on language police. This is not a federalist group, yet they're beginning to realize the truth, while some federalists such as Joe Clark and John Trent have come to show disdain for their own country. They're critical of Canada, but not critical of the Quebec nationalist movement. These people are misguided, and I think I have a solution for them.

I would like to take five dollars of my own money and send it to Professor Trent, to buy him a membership in the Parti Québécois, where he would be most welcome. Their arguments against Canada and his arguments against Canada are identical. Perhaps then, he would be more comfortable with the PQ. Because the rest of Canada is not going to listen to Professor Trent and agree to twist up a country in order not to have it broken up.

Quebec Lambs

Alliance Quebec, which was established as an anglo rights group, was so meek and mild-mannered that it was nicknamed Compliance Quebec, and dismissed as nothing more than a training camp for members of the Quebec Liberal Party. After the referendum, though, even the Alliance realized that if it wanted to hold on to any of its constituency, it had to adopt a more "militant" approach. It decided to stage a rally to protest voter fraud. Only in Canada does standing up against electoral fraud cause one to be described as militant.

But it was all too much for the reality-challenged members of the lamb lobby. The lamb lobby does not like the idea of Alliance Quebec getting involved in the unity debate or — heaven forfend — discussing partition, even though that is the preferred option for the majority of anglophones who want to have no part of living in a French republic of

Quebec. Non-francophones know how their rights have been slowly and subtly but surely taken away from them already — without separation and without distinct society status. They can just imagine how well they would be treated under a government led by Parti Québécois hard-liners — a government that would be looking for scapegoats when the going got tough.

Members of the lamb lobby don't like to stand up for their rights. That would be impolite. That might anger the majority, and if they get angry at us they might take away more of our rights. This view was certainly validated by Deputy Premier Bernard Landry, who threatened that if anglos did annoy the majority by standing up for their rights, those rights might just have to be "re-examined."

The lamb lobby may have been frightened, but ever since the watershed partition rally that attracted 1,200 people to McGill University in January 1996, the catchphrase of loyal Canadians living in Quebec has been "Enough is enough." These are not "extremists." They are people who have decided that in order to get respect, you don't crawl and you don't beg. You get up off your knees and proclaim that French Canadians are no better and no worse than anyone else. The rights of an anglophone are just as important as the rights of a francophone. That is one hell of a new concept in Quebec, but it's about time it started becoming a reality.

Members of the lamb lobby are not at all pleased by these developments. They have been down for so long, they no longer remember which way is up. Lamb lobbyists much prefer the old Alliance Quebec. *Work quietly behind the scenes. Be discreet. Be humble. Be reasonable. Build bridges. Compromise. Get on your knees and beg, and maybe you will be tossed a bone.*

Whatever you do, the lamb lobbyists plead, *don't rock the boat. Don't get the ruling class angry. If you insist on your rights, you might annoy them and you certainly wouldn't want that to happen right in the middle of our bridge-building.*

The lamb lobbyists are wrong. It's time to stop cowering in the shadows. It's time to rock the boat. It's time to take a lesson from the separatists. They are not shy at all about stating their case, and they are ready to rock the entire country.

Members of the lamb lobby are labouring under the delusion that the Quebec government will do something about English health and social services, youth employment, and civil service hiring if Alliance Quebec commissions a few studies and submits some position papers.

Like hell it will. The Quebec government will respect our rights only when we start standing up for them.

The Will of the People
versus the Rule of Law

The chief premise of the lamb lobby is that there is widespread dissatisfaction among French Quebecers with the current system, and that this large group must be placated at any cost. To them, the end justifies the means, and the end in this case, as they see it, is "preserving the social peace," regardless of whether or not it is based on *justice*.

First of all, it is important for people to understand that while separatist sentiment is high within Quebec, its support has been exaggerated. There are only two million hardcore separatists in the province, a large number when taken on its own, but considerably less than half of the overall picture in Quebec. In the last referendum, 60 percent of francophones voted Yes, 40 percent voted No. There are six million francophones living in Quebec. Forty percent of six million is 2.4 million people who voted No. These French Canadians voted against separation despite the fact that it was so easy for them to vote Yes. That's how attached they are to Canada.

It's important to repeat this: the response to the previous referendum on sovereignty in 1980 was No; the response in 1995 again was No. And in 1980, the substance of the question was, "Would you give the government of Quebec a mandate to negotiate some sort of arrangement with Canada?" Sixty percent said, in effect, "No, we don't even want you to negotiate anything."

Last October, 50.6 percent said No, even though if you were French Canadian it made no sense to vote No, because you had nothing to lose — especially if you were basing your vote on what you saw on television three or four days before the referendum. What you saw, on one hand, was the prime minister lowered to the level of begging, and, on the other hand, Lucien Bouchard proudly giving two different speeches — one diplomatic for the rest of Canada, and one full of venom and hatred to drum up support in Quebec.

When people look at the close results in the last referendum and say, "Boy, we really underestimated the dissatisfaction of people in Quebec," they're drawing precisely the wrong conclusion. The reason it came so close the last time is because is was so damn *easy* to vote Yes. The separatists told the people they'd have a Canadian passport, Canadian citizenship, an economic deal, a political deal — absolutely everything. The separatists basically said, "Listen buddy, the day after a Yes vote, in order to reassure financial markets, Jean Chrétien's going to have to pose for a picture with Lucien Bouchard, shaking hands and telling the international community, "Hey, don't worry. We'll just re-jig this thing and everything will be just fine.' "

If that were the true vision, of course people should vote Yes. Last time, there was no point in voting No, because the Canadian government didn't seriously contradict a single part of the separatist vision.

But there's another side to the separatist vision, a downside which so few people talk about: the separatists ignore 3.5 million federalists who live in Quebec, and who have rights as Canadians as guaranteed under the charter. They would have had their country, their birthright, stolen from them based on a trick question and an illegal declaration by the National Assembly.

And they aren't the only ones who would have felt betrayed. Of the 2.5 million Quebecers who voted Yes, one million were so confused that they honestly thought they'd still send MPs to Ottawa, and that they would still maintain their Canadian passports — in essence, they were under the delusion that nothing would change.

But whose fault is that? The sovereignists? Absolutely not. They say everything possible to win, and they'll lie, cheat, cajole, trick, and generally do whatever it takes to get people to vote Yes. And, in order to be successful, what they need more than anything is for the federalist morons in Ottawa to sit by and not contradict anything. Because if the federalists don't contradict their claims, these claims become the accepted wisdom, and they enter the realm of mythology — which is what rules the day for Quebec nationalists.

But let's leave aside the very important fact that the people have spoken and have voted in favour of remaining in Canada, not once but twice. Let's say that perhaps the next time around the sovereignists will be able to manipulate the vote to come out to 50 percent plus one in favour of separation. We still need to know where we stand in terms of the law.

Some lamb lobbyists have gone so far as to say the law really doesn't matter. In an editorial published last summer, Joan Fraser, former editor-in-chief at the *Gazette*, wrote, "What matters most — indeed, more than any law — is the true democratic will of the people of the province."

This is outrageous, because it is simply not true. What if

the people have the will to enslave the rest of Canada? The Quebec government could put forth a referendum question such as, "Would you like the rest of Canada to become your slaves?" and they might get a 52-percent Yes response, especially if they added, "And they would be responsible for paying all of your taxes." But that doesn't mean they could do it, because slavery is against the law, and stealing is against the law. So the notion that the will of the people is more important than any law is not only incorrect, it's extremely dangerous.

The will of the people is *subject* to the law. That's what Joan Fraser should have said. If the people want to separate, they can. But *within the law.* We live in a law-abiding society, and the only alternative to living under a set of laws is anarchy. And no one — not federalists, not sovereignists — is interested in living in an atmosphere of anarchy.

The sovereignists don't like the idea of their attempt to break up this country being subject to any laws other than the ones they make up themselves in order to achieve their goal. Fairness has nothing to do with it. Lucien Bouchard has never been even remotely interested in asking an honest question in a referendum, otherwise he would have asked the voters, "Do you want Quebec to be a separate (or independent) country from Canada?" He won't ask that question because he knows what the answer would be. He knows the basic truth, that the overwhelming majority of Quebecers are still attached to Canada, and that they have absolutely no intention of separating, of becoming an independent country. That's why the separatists have to ask these trick questions offering Quebecers a partnership with Canada. And they can't even ask these trick questions only once or twice; they have to keep asking the trick questions, because the answer is still always a resounding No.

Joan Fraser was only following the reasoning of federal Justice Minister Allan Rock, who had said that, yes, a unilateral declaration of independence may be unconstitutional and therefore against the law, but that's only a technicality. He has changed his tune since.

That comment was more outrageous than what Fraser said. This is a justice minister saying that the rule of law is a technicality. According to this logic, I can rob a bank, and then, when I'm confronted with the fact that it's against the law to steal, I can respond, "Well, yeah, but that's only a technicality. What's important here is that I need the money. My will and the will of my accomplices in the getaway car was decided by way of a democratic vote, within the car. The four of us decided that we should rob this bank. And we have excellent reasons for it. We're broke and our families need the money. So we should have the right, under such circumstances, to break the law."

It's the exact same thing to allow the sovereignists to decide to break up Canada, based on their democratic vote, in their own region, all the while insisting that the fact that it's against the law is irrelevant. This is an absurdity that the federal government has let the separatists get away with time and again. Allan Rock let them get away with it. The lamb lobby lets them get away with it. That's why a reality check is so important. We have to say, "No. The rule of law applies. You'll have to deal with it."

Is this inconvenient for the separatists? You bet it is. It's much more difficult to separate legally than illegally, because if it's decided upon legally, then there are some kind of constraints. They'd rather not have the constraints. They'd rather catch the populace in a bad mood because of some jurisdictional dispute, and then, *bang!*, get 50 percent plus one, break up the country, and expect the rest of Canada to sit by and applaud.

The Nihilist Left

While the vast majority of Canadians will not applaud the breakup of their country, there are those who couldn't even be bothered to care. These are people who, if they pay any attention to the debate over separation at all, sit on the sidelines sniping, criticizing, snickering, and condemning. Some might call them the far left or the loony left, but I prefer to call them nihilists, because they're willing to throw away their own birthright, all because they think they're above it all.

Among the nihilists is Peter Scowen, the former editor of the *Montreal Mirror*, who regards the whole national unity debate as a tacky preoccupation of the "establishment," and that, far from being important, all it involves is flag waving.

Why can't the nihilists be bothered to support their own country against the threat of separation? Because they cling to an antiquated notion that French Canadians are among the "oppressed peoples" of the world. This is an absurdity, of course, and you can tell how absurd it is when you present it to any foreign audience, and they ask, "Well, how are French Canadians oppressed?"

If you're honest, your answer goes something like, "Well, they don't have control over some jurisdictions, but they get to be prime minister as well as leader of the opposition, they get to run the country, their language is one of the two official languages of the country, yet they can bar English from the province of Quebec and make French the only official language, and they can bar English from public signs. That's how they are oppressed."

It's a preposterous notion, but nonetheless many leftists feel that the Québécois are an oppressed minority, and that they are involved in a laudable struggle for national liberation. Somehow, they seem to have missed out on a crucial point. No oppressed minority gets to *run* the country.

Period. It's unprecedented. It's a contradiction in terms. *If you're an oppressed minority, you can't run the country.* This fact has been lost on the nihilists.

As for Quebecers not being given full respect, that may have been a real problem thirty or forty years ago, but it has since changed. It changed because anglophones went along with those changes, and no one's questioning that the changes should have occurred. Furthermore, it was never the fault of the anglophone community that, for generations, the Catholic church kept francophones down and told them they shouldn't be involved in business, and that they shouldn't go to school other than to become priests.

Previous injustices — *long since corrected* — are not reason enough to break up this country. And in case you need proof that the situation in Quebec has changed for francophones, just walk down any street in Montreal. The city is more French now than it ever was. Why are we discussing the arguments of 1955 as we approach the twenty-first century? Is this payback? Is it revenge? And are we supposed to go along with this revenge against us for a crime we did not commit?

Here is an example of how the loony leftist mindset perceives Canada as the oppressor and Quebec as the victim. When Pierre Trudeau responded to separatist terrorism in Montreal by invoking the War Measures Act in October 1970, a local broadcaster began his radio address with these words: "I went to bed in a democracy and woke up in a police state."

Obviously, this man never lived in a police state, so he wouldn't recognize one if he tripped over it. If he thinks that three tanks guarding a couple of political leaders, with no one being shot and no one being killed, and the number of injuries being zero, constitutes a police state, then he clearly hasn't a clue as to what a police state really is. Because the score, in terms of how many murders were committed, was

Separatists 1, Federalists 0. Canada is neither a prison nor a police state today, and it wasn't one in 1970, either.

How do I know this? Because I have plenty of experience with a police state, having been born in Hungary before immigrating to Canada in 1956. I distinctly recall being five years old, going for a walk with my father, and seeing police officers hanging from the trees dead. Now *that* was a police state.

I was an eyewitness to serious repression. So, in 1970, at the age of nineteen, when I heard that remark on the radio, I said to myself, "Well, this doesn't seem like a police state to me. No one's been injured and no one's been killed" — except, of course, by the criminals of the Front de Libé-ration du Québec (FLQ), who have now, of course, been elevated to hero status and invited to teach. That's right. To this day, the far left continues to excuse FLQ violence as a legitimate response to what they perceived as oppression. These terrorists are now widely hailed as freedom fighters and revolutionaries. The murder of Pierre Laporte has been sanitized in French textbooks: apparently, he just "died" of natural causes in the back of that car.

The nihilists are also under the impression that the separatist movement is a social democratic movement, which is quite a howl, indeed. But not that it hasn't been used by Lucien Bouchard and Jacques Parizeau. "Oh, the Winds of Right-Wing Change blowing from Alberta and Ontario will never come to Quebec," they told the people of Quebec.

That's true. Because the right-wing change here is worse. Even Ralph Klein wouldn't have mentally ill patients having to choose between paying for their medication or paying for food.

At least Ralph Klein and Mike Harris had the decency to say they were going to run on a cost-cutting program before they got elected. Mike Harris didn't say he was a social democrat. He said, "I'm going to come in and I'm going to cut welfare." The people voted him in and what did he do? He cut welfare. On the other hand, Lucien Bouchard's line — "Oh, no cuts for us; we believe in these programs" — has turned out to be a complete lie. They've been slashing away at subsidies for medicine for the elderly.

It has been the most vicious attack on the weak in our society, on the mentally ill, the poor, and the impoverished, elderly welfare recipients. We have no money to help the most vulnerable members of our society pay for their medication, but we do have money for sovereignty studies. This is the contradiction of Quebec, and it never gets noted by those who claim that independence would result in a more just and compassionate society.

Occasionally, probably out of wishful thinking, someone will try to claim that the Parti Québécois is more compassionate towards the weak in society than are the Liberals, who have the nerve to be supported by — Oh dear! — Big Business. "After all," these people reason, "René Lévesque founded the party along social democratic principles." Yet, even this is stretching at the truth. Back in the 1970s, the PQ told the unions, "Listen, you help us and we'll do everything we can for you." The unions lived up to their end of the bargain, but the PQ soon rolled back union salaries by 20 percent. They robbed them blind.

The PQ have a history of backing off from their promises, and now they've proved it beyond a shadow of a doubt. They've shafted women in terms of pay equity, and now they've shafted the elderly, they've shafted welfare recipients, and they've shafted the mentally handicapped. That's just for starters. It's barely been a year since the referendum. Just you wait.

Welfare recipients are being attacked in Alberta, in Ontario, and in Quebec. What is untouchable in Quebec, though, is language and culture. There's plenty of money for language police but not for medication, because Quebec is a distinct society, and our priorities are different. Our priorities are not people, not health, not welfare, but language, culture, discrimination against our minorities. Those are the priorities of Quebec.

But the nihilists persist, critical of everything anyone might do to try to keep this country together.

The chief meeting ground for the nihilists is in the pages of the alternative press, dominated by people who think they're above the whole debate. Even though they'll concede that it makes a certain amount of sense to be federalist, because they understand the dangers of nationalism, they don't like their bedfellows if it means they're saying the same thing that the prime minister of the country is. *How can an alternative newspaper be on the side of the prime minister? Why, it's a contradiction in terms.* So, they figure to themselves, whoever else is against the prime minister has to be on to something. And, as a result, they are tacitly in bed with the separatists.

But, fortunately, the number of leftists who think that separation is a great idea is diminishing. First of all, there are fewer leftists around. And even the ones who are committed to it realize that separation is not compatible with social democracy. That's why the NDP has never gotten anywhere in Quebec. Nationalist fervour is a far more potent force in Quebec than is concern for the downtrodden. Especially these days, when the people who are downtrodden in Quebec are the minorities and the anglophones. Not francophones. Nor are francophones downtrodden in Canada either. Ottawa is the home of French power. French Canadians run the country. How can a downtrodden people run the country?

Within Quebec there are poor anglophones and poor francophones, but francophones have a much better chance of getting a job in Quebec than anglophones do. The

Quebec civil service is 97 percent pure French Canadian Catholic. That's the truth of it, politically incorrect though it may be to say. That's the way it was five years ago, ten years ago, fifteen years ago, twenty years ago. They said it was terrible and that it would change. Has it changed? Of course not. Why hasn't it changed? Because they don't want it to change. It's as simple as that. They don't have to issue any government directive, that's just the feeling there is.

Let's not forget Jacques Parizeau's speech. Everybody remembers the words "money" and "ethnics"; everybody forgets the word "revenge," which he used several times. Part of the revenge is, if you're a hiring officer in a personnel office, you hire French Canadians. You don't hire a person who is likely to have voted No.

The Real Issues

The nihilists' line of reasoning is that this constant "bickering" and "quibbling" over separation is just a diversion from the "real issues" of social justice and poverty, violence against women, and so on, that plague our society.

First of all, while these other issues are vitally important, we can walk and chew gum at the same time. It's not like we have to choose one over the other.

Secondly, we can't just *get over* this issue. Even if we tried to put this issue to the side, it wouldn't just *go* to the side. Nor is the question of national unity irrelevant to us on a direct, everyday level. Every single Canadian has to pay more in mortgage rates and more in their credit card rates, and Canada has to pay higher interest rates for borrowing because of the political uncertainty in Quebec. This is literally taking money out of the hands of welfare mothers, because money that could be used for social programs is used to pay higher interest payments — all because this issue has never been settled once and for all.

It's not going to be an easy issue to settle, but caving in constantly has proven to be ineffective for decades.

The nihilists claim to be tired of this debate. Fair enough. Most Canadians are damn near exhausted from it. But the answer is not to simply throw up your hands and say, "Why not just get it over with?" You don't just break up a country when the vast majority of the population are quite satisfied with it. You don't sacrifice a country when 90 percent are happy with it as compared with 10 percent who are grumbling.

The lamb lobby also claims to be tired of the debate. They too want to get on with the so-called real issues of the day. Flag waving, demanding our rights — these are all some sort of tacky sideshow in their view. "It's the economy, stupid!" is their latest refrain. We need to stop wasting our energy on things such as sign laws and the threat of separation, they reason. Instead, we should all pull together and fix the Quebec economy.

That's like saying, "Let's forget about the fact that there's a pink elephant in the room and discuss something else." Well, you *can't* do anything while there's a pink elephant in the room, because there's no room to move.

"It's the economy, stupid!" is basically Lucien Bouchard's argument. He's essentially saying, "Forget that I am damaging the economy; let's fix the economy." We *can't* forget that he's the one who's damaging the economy. We can't forget that it's the separatist movement that is causing the problem in the first place.

Why are almost all of the other provinces across Canada doing better economically than Quebec? Why is the U.S. economy doing so incredibly well? They've got their own set of problems, but they don't have to live under this ridiculous, never-ending threat. *Let's forget about separation? Let's put it on the back burner while we work on other important matters such as the economy?* How can the prospect of the country breaking apart be on the back burner?!

The message should be, "It's the threat of separation, stupid!" That's the number one problem with the economy. Most economists will tell you that. You'll only hear about the one or two economists who say that separation is a great thing, though. The ones who tell you otherwise are mostly ignored in the Quebec media.

Committed Federalists

The vast majority of people in this country — and I count myself among them — are committed federalists. Unlike the elites, most of whom see nothing wrong with saying Canada is not good enough for Quebec as it is, committed federalists believe that if Canada has its problems, those problems are not at its constitutional core.

The Canadian Constitution grants equality for all citizens before the law. Period.

To the conditional federalist, who never tires of threatening us with the breakup of our country if we don't do all we can to accommodate a *minority* within one of our regions, the staunch federalist is a nightmare. Such a person is unwilling to bend on a few small issues. Unwilling to sacrifice a few of his or her own rights for the greater good of keeping this country together.

To the committed federalist, though, this trade-off is unacceptable. What good is preserving a country that won't stand up for the rights of *all* its citizens? What exactly is the point in preserving a country that is universally hailed as the greatest place in the world in which to live, and where people have gotten along very well for 130 years, *if that country won't stand up for itself?*

Those who would try to keep the country together by

selling out the rights of its minorities think of themselves as practical and realistic. They are most certainly *not* realistic, because their strategy of appeasement is doomed to failure.

What these conditional federalists *are* is cynical.

Remember that the next time you find yourself under attack from one of these cynics. They regard you as a nuisance because you believe that Canada is more than just a convenience. You believe that Canada stands for certain values. Those values are enshrined in the Constitution, which says that Canada is a pluralistic, open, and tolerant society. It is a document which recognizes that we are a nation of immigrants. And it also says that we are a nation with two official languages, French and English.

If these values are not worth standing up for, if they're worth throwing away for the sole purpose of pleasing those who want to tear the country apart, then what's the point of continuing to believe in this nation?

Anglophone Hardliners

If you live anywhere in Canada outside Quebec, speak English, and do not support recognizing Quebec in the Constitution as a distinct society, then you've probably heard yourself described by the elites as a redneck and a small-minded bigot. Maybe they'll question your patriotism, accusing you of being willing to flush Canada down the drain, all for your own selfish, stubborn attitudes. You're a simpleton, too dimwitted to go along with your leaders and endorse a series of convoluted solutions to problems too "complex" for you to understand.

Above all, you are just too provincial, too insular for your elites, who will tell you that you "just don't understand Quebec."

Don't worry. You're not alone.

Within Quebec, federalists committed to preserving Canada as it is are called extremists. Because we *do* "understand Quebec" and are worried about our rights in a sovereign Quebec, and because we believe passionately in the Constitution which protects the rights of all Canadian citizens, we are called anglophone hardliners.

For the lamb lobby, the problem with us is that we're so darn bad at public relations. We're an embarrassment. We're not putting on our most attractive face. We're not flexible enough.

We, on the other hand, feel that Canada doesn't need a slick PR campaign to be made appealing for Quebecers. Canada *is* the public relations. The lamb lobby has not had the decency to stand up for this country and say how much it has done for Quebecers.

As for being an anglophone hardliner, I have 40 percent of French Quebecers standing alongside me, who feel the same attachment to Canada as I do. That's not what the lamb lobby concentrates on. The lambs are so out of touch with reality that they are obsessed with pleasing the 10 percent of Quebecers who are soft nationalists, while ignoring the 40 percent of francophones who are staunch Canadian federalists.

We've gotten so far that if you stand up for Canada, you're called an anglophone hardliner, intransigent and not understanding of Quebec's uniqueness. This is absolute, utter drivel, because, let me repeat, 40 percent of francophones feel very strongly attached to Canada. They don't think the National Assembly should have the right to break up this country; they don't think the separatists should have the right to set the agenda. They desperately want the federal government to stand up for Canada. These are not just anglophones but 2.4 million *francophones*. Forty percent of Quebec francophones were even in favour of partition, for heaven's sake, because they do not want to live under an ethnocentric regime, which is what they would be guaranteed in an independent Quebec.

We will never do anything to convince separatists that Canada is a great country. We should stop trying to convince them of anything. It's a fantastic country, and if they don't realize it, that's their problem. They'll have to deal with it. They just can't hijack others to go along with breaking apart something that they don't like.

The more you go along with the lamb lobby's policy of doing everything possible to please some of the sovereignists, the more you are validating the separatist-painted picture of a Canada that is not good enough for Quebec, that has been unfair to Quebec, that has oppressed Quebec, that has humiliated Quebec. This picture is a lie, and it must be exposed for the lie it is. You can't force people to believe in Canada or not to believe in it, but at least the lie should be pointed out.

As for the public relations campaign of the lamb lobby, of showing how flexible we Canadians are — we have been doing that PR campaign for thirty years, and it has not worked at all. It didn't work in the past, it won't work in the future, it doesn't work with teenagers, and it doesn't work with nations. It is a strategy of appeasement, which tells Quebecers, in essence, "We agree with you, this country isn't good enough. What can we do to make you feel more comfortable?"

We have got to stop this sort of defensiveness, because we have already bent over backwards to make all Canadians comfortable. This is the crucial point, and one that should be told to the lamb lobby over and over again: twenty-eight million Canadians feel comfortable, thank you very much, *in Canada*. They feel welcome. Two million don't.

Now those two million, what a coincidence, happen to be the same people who want to build a separate French country, with notions of *exclusion*, not of *inclusion*, with a notion of intolerance for anybody who isn't francophone, not a notion of tolerance. Canada wants to be *bi*lingual, Quebec wants to be *uni*lingual. Canada passes laws to *promote* French, Quebec passes laws to *downgrade* English.

That is the difference. And we forget constantly about the twenty-eight million, and keep harping on the two million, whose stated goal is the breakup of this country. And again, we always keep coming back to the 2.4 million French Canadians who also do not feel part of the Quebec "nation." They feel part of the Canadian nation living in the province of Quebec. And the opinion of those 2.4 million people is not represented by Lucien Bouchard, is not represented by Daniel Johnson, and is not represented by Jean Chrétien.

These 2.4 million francophone federalists have no voice speaking for them. Absolutely none. Their voice has been silenced. They don't speak up too much because it isn't politically correct to be French Canadian and a federalist. It may not be politically correct, but there are 2.4 million people who hold this politically incorrect view, and it's about time they got some support from the rest of Canada. The way to get that support is for the people in the rest of Canada to tell their representatives in Ottawa that *We remember those 2.4 million French Canadians who are federalists and want to stay in Canada. When dealing with Quebec, don't forget to keep them in mind as well.*

Tell your MPs that you aren't interested in a tribal nationalist worldview. Remind them that Canada works, and that the proof is in the pudding. French and English Canadians have gotten along very well for 130 years. And remind them once again, because they need to hear it: twenty-eight million members of this political nation that was created in 1867 still believe in this country and its vision as outlined in the Constitution.

Lucien Bouchard is saying that Canada doesn't work. He's lying, because twenty-eight million people — the overwhelming *democratic* majority of the Canadian people — think it *does* work, including 2.4 million French Canadians living in Quebec.

Wanted: Strong Federalist Leaders

There are a number of prominent committed federalists on the national scene, people in positions of influence. As soon as we find out their names, we'll tell you. When it comes to national unity, the Reform Party seems to have the right idea. In the media, some highly influential figures include media-mogul Conrad Black, *Financial Post* editor-in-chief Diane Francis, and *Gazette* columnist William Johnson.

These are people who believe in providing Quebecers with a reality check, and they often meet with scorn and derision from the lamb lobbyists, who plead on behalf of so-called moderation. But the lambs' message is ringing increasingly hollow with federalists within Quebec. They've tried moderation, and it failed. While they were being moderate, while they went along with encroachments upon their liberties, with Bill 101 and 300,000 people leaving the province, Quebec nationalists voted against Charlottetown, they sent separatists to the House of Commons, they voted for the Parti Québécois, and they voted in favour of the Yes option during the last referendum. All of this happened while the anglophones were good little anglophones and kept quiet. Did that help the situation or make it worse? Clearly, it made it much worse.

But at the federal level, politicians who have what it takes to stand up to the separatists and tell the truth to Quebecers are few and far between.

The closest person to the right person is Stéphane Dion. When he came out and said, "If Canada is divisible then so is Quebec," the separatists were literally quaking with fear.

Lucien Bouchard is terrified of the notion of partition; that's why he doesn't want to deal with it. He knows that if that subject is on the table, support for sovereignty will plummet.

Stéphane Dion is the first publicly elected figure to hint at a reality check for the separatists, and I applaud him for that. Furthermore, he once had the guts to go to a Quebec Liberal Party convention and tell them straight to their faces that they were undermining the federation. He didn't care about winning any popularity awards, and for his honesty, the Quebec Liberals vowed never to have him back again.

So far, so good.

The bad news is he's still trying to sell us distinct society status for Quebec. He's said that even though it's an old idea and that it's not original, he sees it as Canada's best — and last — chance to keep the country together.

To persuade people of this nonsense, he has to lie. He tells the rest of Canada that it has no meaning, even as he knows perfectly well that Quebec nationalists wouldn't be interested in something that is meaningless. So, finally we have a prominent national politician who has the courage to tell the truth about the costs and consequences of separation, and the daring to tell the Quebec Liberals to smarten up and get with the program, reduced to being dishonest with Canada, as he tries to pass off distinct society as the one and only thing that will save the country.

This is the sad reality of Canadian politicians. Most of them either just don't get it, or they get it but become corrupted by the system. They become convinced that they have to fix everything, and that they in fact *can* fix everything. But they just don't understand that national unity isn't something to be *managed*. Distinct society and other such gimmicks aren't what will save Canada. The Canadian people will save this country. The federal government and federal and provincial politicians throughout this land continually underestimate just how much millions of people in this country really love and are attached to Canada. Though they may not wave the flag as much as Americans or go in for U.S.-style jingoism, they still love this country, and never more so than when they almost lost it.

Canadians became extremely patriotic on October 30, 1995, and that's why I refer to this date as the birth of patriotism in Canada.

PART 3

APPEASEMENT AND WHY IT WILL NEVER WORK

The one message that comes through loud and clear in all of the national unity debates that have been going on for so many years is that the rest of Canada simply does not understand Quebec. Many Canadians are frustrated at this, because they feel that Quebec already gets far more than its share in Confederation. More money. More equalization payments. Certainly more power in Ottawa.

Does it make a difference? Quebec remains the spoiled child of Confederation. Nothing is ever enough and everything is always a humiliation. We give our Olympic athletes a certain amount of money. There's some obscure francophone games in Madagascar, and the athletes going to those receive four or five times as much money. Montreal didn't need a second airport back in the 1970s, yet to appease Quebec, the federal government built Mirabel at a cost of a billion dollars. Now that it has become clear that Mirabel is a white elephant, Bloc Québécois leader Michel Gauthier blames it all on Ottawa!

And get this: In order to help out Quebec, Ottawa places government buildings across the border in the city of Hull,

Quebec, instead of in Ottawa, which is the capital. They put these buildings inside the Quebec border to help revitalize Hull. They put tens of millions of dollars into government buildings and create tens of thousands of jobs in Hull.

Sound generous?

Josée Legault in an editorial in *Le Devoir* entitled "Ein Reich, Ein Volk, Ein Flag" describes the Canadian unity rallies as akin to Nazi Germany and says that the government offices, draped in their oppressive maple leaf flags, constitute an "occupation" of Hull. So when Canada gives tens of millions of dollars to Hull as a gift, the name of the gift is an "occupation." Quebec is being "occupied" by the rest of Canada.

It's a free country, and Josée Legault can spout whatever she likes. But the fact that we allow all this nonsense to go unchecked makes it acceptable to so many people in Quebec, and that is the great tragedy.

Because deep down, the people of Quebec aren't the ones who feel this hostility to Canada; it is the nationalist elite who run the province and who control the levers of power. The people allow them to get away with their demagoguery. But they only succeed to the extent that Canada remains silent. If the federal government hopes to gain ground in Quebec, it must take a more active role in the national unity debate. What that means is spelling the issue out clearly for Quebecers.

There are two options for those who want to keep Quebec in Canada. The first of these options is known as Plan A, and it is the one Canada has been trying for decades with no success whatsoever. According to Plan A, Canada allows Quebec to call all the shots for splitting the country apart. *Have as many referendums as you want*, says the A-team. *There's nothing we can do about that. And no, we understand, in the event of a Yes vote, what the people say is binding — for all of us. We'd prefer to stay in Canada, we'll vote to stay in*

Canada, but we'll accept whatever the separatists tell us to accept. We certainly wouldn't want to make a fuss and draw attention to ourselves.

Well, if that's the route we go, the separatists will eventually win. And once they do, we will all be the poorer for it. Yet for some reason Plan A is the only plan that's ever been on the table. It's not even a plan. It's the equivalent of throwing your hands up in the air and saying, "Ah, you take care of it. Just leave us out of it."

The second option — Plan B — is really the only alternative to this suicidal compliance. It's time for Canada to stand up for its own interests and present all Quebecers with a *reality check*. Canada must do everything possible to ensure that everyone knows exactly what they're getting into *before* they vote either for independence or to remain in Canada. Plan B means Canada forcing the issue and saying, "Let's sit down at the table and discuss what will be the costs and consequences of separation."

Unfortunately, at the moment, most federal politicians and their allies in the chattering classes favour Plan A, if only because they're so used to it.

Plan A-for-Appeasement

The people who support this approach are those who honestly feel that the best way to keep Canada together is to beg and bribe Quebec to stay. Nothing, however, could be further from the truth. These people may be well-intentioned, but they are absolutely wrong. Not only will this process not help, it will hinder.

Appeasement simply does not do the job. It did not work with Germany in the events leading up to the Second World War. And it will not work with Quebec. What it *will* do is lend credence to the basic separatist tenet that there is

CANADA IS NOT A REAL COUNTRY

something seriously wrong with this country.

Let me repeat it one more time: there is nothing seriously wrong with this country.

There *is*, however, something seriously wrong with letting a group of nationalists with a chip on their shoulder set the agenda for twenty-eight million Canadians who feel very attached to this country and do not want to see it broken apart.

We must stop trying to fix Canada so that Quebec nationalists will learn to love it. They will never love it until they destroy it. We must stop playing on their playing field and we must stop the madness of allowing them to set the agenda.

Plan A hinges on one simple — and fatally flawed — proposal: amending the Constitution to recognize Quebec as a distinct society within Canada.

Distinct Society

Distinct society has got to be one of the most divisive issues ever in Canadian politics. The people don't like it, though most of their politicians do.

Former Newfoundland premier Clyde Wells was one of the most respected politicians in all of Canada, a man of honesty and integrity. What was his great sin? He dared to say that all Canadians should be treated equal. This was too much for the establishment politicians in Canada. *Outrageous! Get him out of here.* That's where we've gotten to. In order to appease Quebec, a man who held the perfectly reasonable position that Quebec should have no special privileges within confederation — it can protect its language and culture, but it can't take away the rights of others — was considered an extremist and literally driven out of politics.

Outside of Quebec, the strongest opponents of a distinct society constitutional amendment since day one have been British Columbia and Alberta, and there is no sign that the people of these provinces are about to change their minds. We may not know where Alberta premier Ralph Klein stands on the issue — first he was against distinct society, then he came to Quebec and had lunch with a francophone and seemed to change his mind — but it really doesn't matter one way or the other. The people of Alberta don't care about who he had lunch with. They don't feel that Albertans ought to have any fewer rights than their fellow Canadians living in Quebec, and vice versa.

The premier of British Columbia, Glen Clark, has made his position clear. He understands his constituents, and knows how they feel about distinct society status, so he's not going to try ramming it down their throats. And deep down, Ralph Klein knows the same holds true for his own province. For all practical purposes, it's over.

But distinct society status for Quebec is like Canada's version of *The Undead*. We need to put a stake through the heart of those two words to kill the concept once and for all. Sovereignists in Quebec don't like it, federalists in the West don't like it. The concept is of no interest to anyone. But still, the political and media elites persist, trying to convince Canadians that these two words that mean different things to different people, depending on where they live, are Canada's last and best chance of keeping the country united.

In a May 29, 1996, editorial, the *Toronto Star* declared, "Canada won't hang together on feel good platitudes. Quebecers want real change and in the Constitution."

Quebecers want real change all right. Separatist Quebecers want to break up Canada. Federalist Quebecers want Ottawa to for once stand up for the rights of the twenty-eight million Canadians who do not want to see this country broken apart.

Quebecers who are separatists, on the other hand, want their own country and they couldn't care less about the Constitution. The separatists have stated in no uncertain terms, time and time again, that a Yes vote will allow the National Assembly to proclaim a unilateral declaration of independence, thus throwing the Canadian Constitution and Canadian law into the garbage against the wishes of half of the population of Quebec. That the Quebec Liberals go along with this same basic philosophy only proves one thing — that the future of Canada cannot be left in the hands of Daniel Johnson.

The *Star* editorial says that last October's referendum message was that Quebecers want Canada to accommodate them by altering its Constitution. That was *not* the referendum message. Far from it. The referendum message was that, despite the trick question, the stolen votes, and the pathetic performance of the federal government, the majority of Quebecers do not want to be part of a separate country. That message was ignored by the separatist government, which is determined to hold as many referendums as it takes until they get the answer they want. That's understandable, but for federalists to go along with their reasoning is absurd.

The *Star* editorial actually said that Ontario premier Mike Harris "could warm Quebecers' hearts, undercut Bouchard and deal separatism a blow with one simple declaration: Ontario supports changing the Canadian Constitution to recognize Quebec as a distinct society."

How wrong can you get?

This Hallmark greeting card logic baffles me. While editorialists are trying to find ways to warm Quebecers' hearts, the separatists are contemplating their next move in their plan to unilaterally break up Canada.

How much more can we compromise than we have now? What can we possibly do? We have come as close as we can to Quebec being a separate country. We're an inch away from it already, so what more is there to compromise? What could we possibly do further that would be acceptable to Lucien Bouchard?

Nothing. He said it clearly at the press conference where he accepted the leadership of the Parti Québécois. There's no compromise we can offer, because we've been told in advance that no compromise is acceptable. The separatists are honest about that, and I admire that bit of honesty. There is no compromise acceptable, because what staunch Quebec nationalists want is to have their own country. And you can't have your own country and stay part of another country at the same time.

Isn't Distinct Society Just a Statement of the Obvious?

All of the salesmen who try to sell this lousy product known as distinct society will try to tell you that all it means is that we recognize that Quebec is French. *Since we know that already, there's no big deal. It's merely a statement of the obvious, a statement of fact.*

But that's *not* all that it is.

Look in the dictionary. Distinct means "separate." What better definition could separatists want?

Brian Mulroney tried to ram it down everyone's throat at Meech Lake. There was no support for Meech in public opinion polls, but it was Manitoba and Newfoundland, thank God, that signalled the death knell for the accord.

A few years later, the concept resurfaced as part of the Charlottetown Accord and was put to a vote in a national referendum. Quebec itself voted 57 percent against the accord — meaning, the people of Quebec said *No* to distinct society. The accord was supported in the Maritimes and in

Ontario, where it came in at a dead heat, but was defeated overwhelmingly in the western provinces. The voters in Quebec didn't want it because they thought it was not enough, while the voters in the West didn't want it because they thought it was too much. But all that Charlottetown proved is that distinct society settles nothing.

After its overwhelming rejection by Canada, distinct society was dead in the water. Who resuscitated it? The two No leaders, Daniel Johnson and Jean Chrétien.

Initially, during the run-up to the October referendum, the two of them had agreed that this was not a constitutional referendum and thus had nothing to do with distinct society. It was about whether Quebec was to separate or not. Then, in a last-minute panic caused by their own ineptitude in the referendum campaign, the Quebec Liberals said, "If we don't have distinct society, it's over." They tricked Jean Chrétien. He had to promise to push for it, and now he's stuck with a notion he can't sell, and that he doesn't believe in, because it in effect creates two classes of citizens.

So, here we have the prime minister of Canada promoting a divisive concept that he doesn't believe in, and that has been turned down by the people of Quebec, as well as by the rest of the people in this country.

The two sales department heads are Daniel Johnson and Stéphane Dion. Now, what they say to the rest of Canada is, "Oh, it means nothing. It just means acknowledging a fact that already is."

Well, gee, you'd think. *That sounds simple enough. Why don't we all go along with it? My goodness, is that all it takes? You mean if we say yes to these two words, nothing will change and Canada will be united? Boy, that seems like a terribly cheap price to pay. Let's do it!*

That's how stupid these so-called federalists take the Canadian people for. "It means nothing," they say to Canadians outside Quebec. Of course, when they come here, the spiel is completely different. Over here, it has to have, as Daniel Johnson says, "legal impact." Well, legal impact upon whom? Legal impact to do what?

As we all know, the soft nationalists in Quebec have *never* wanted to discuss specifically what distinct society would be used for. Former justice minister Gil Rémillard, Robert Bourassa's point man on the Constitution during the Meech Lake debate, was repeatedly confronted on it. "We can make this really easy: Why don't you specify what it's going to be used for?" "Oh no," he said back then.

They won't specify because you and I and everyone reading this book knows perfectly well what Quebec wants to use it for: to repress its minority and promote the interests of French Canadians over the interests of everyone else in Quebec, without the humiliation of having to use the notwithstanding clause every time it wants to pass a repressive law.

As if to reassure us, the sales department tells us that the courts would use the distinct society clause to interpret the Canadian Constitution. In other words, if, as an oppressed minority, you went to the Supreme Court of Canada and said, "I've been screwed by this rule," the court could easily say, "I'm sorry, you're right, it's not very fair, and we wouldn't allow it from any of the other nine provinces. But we've all agreed in the Constitution that Quebec is a distinct society, which means it promotes and protects the fact that it's French, and this in turn means that they *can* do whatever they deem appropriate for that purpose. Sorry, sucker. You're screwed."

In Quebec, we're not stupid. We know what it would be used for. What else is the point of it if it "doesn't mean anything"? Why would Quebec want something that means nothing? It wants something that will give it more power to create two classes of citizens.

95

Canada's Last Chance?

When the *Toronto Star* and the conditional federalists through-out Canada start warning you that distinct society is what the people of Quebec want, just remember that they've already voted it down once before. But even if Quebecers suddenly had a change of heart, do you think that would matter to their separatist leaders? Absolutely not.

In 1982, the majority of Quebecers according to all the polls were in favour of patriating the Constitution, and so were seventy-two out of seventy-five Liberal MPs who were duly elected by the people of Quebec. But the opinion of the people of Quebec on that issue did not matter to René Lévesque. He could never have signed any deal, for heaven's sake, because he was a separatist. Separatists do not sign the Canadian Constitution, because they do not want to be part of Canada. That is why they are called separatists.

The Quebec Liberals, led at the time by Claude Ryan, also did not like the idea of being part of the Constitution because, as usual, they were trying to portray themselves as being as nationalist as the next guy. So, in the popular mythology, the only thing that counts is that, in 1982, the "people" of Quebec were "humiliated" and the Constitu-tion was patriated against their will.

It was not against the will of Quebec. It was only against the will of the separatist and quasi-separatist parties of Quebec.

Why do I mention this? Because it illustrates the point that, even if Canada recognized the people of Quebec as a distinct society, what the Quebec people want is irrelevant to their politicians. The separatists don't care what the people want; what the separatists want is separation. But they like Ottawa to continue paying the bill. You can't get better separation than that. That's like leaving home and having your parents pick up the tab.

The national unity debate has been a one-sided debate for years, with Quebec extorting more and more in exchange for nothing, other than agreeing to stay for the moment. If Quebec were recognized as a distinct society, what is to stop separatist politicians from holding yet another referendum two or three years down the road on some other trumped up "humiliation?" The Allaire Report, which came not from the separatist party but from the Quebec Liberal Party, threatened separation from Canada unless Quebec was granted control over practically everything but postage stamps and equalization payments.

If distinct society finally were to be accepted by the rest of Canada, what do you think would happen to Lucien Bouchard and the Bloc Québécois and the PQ, to the sovereignist hardliners who have in some cases spent all their lives dreaming of an independent Quebec? Do you think they would give up on the dream and say, "Oh, well. Too bad"?

Absolutely not!

The separatist movement would continue. Lucien Bouchard, the most talented politician this country has seen in decades, would be able to dismiss distinct society recognition as too little, too late and say, "See what happens? Whenever we want something, whenever we threaten to leave, we get more concessions." Robert Bourassa, supposedly a federalist, when trying to sell his people on the Charlottetown Accord, said, "Think of this as the beginning. Think of it as the consolation prize. We'll come back for more later." If by some miracle it were to pass now, do you think Quebec would say, "Thank you for giving us distinct society. We can now be proud Canadians"? A likely story.

All distinct society would do is make things easier for the separatists. Right now, there are not two nations in this country; there is one political nation comprised of English

Canadians, French Canadians, new Canadians, and native peoples, and we have all worked together to successfully build this country. A distinct society will artificially divide us into two categories.

Even without distinct society, Quebec already has *all the power* and *all the rights* to protect its language and culture to the extent that it can abolish English as one of the official languages. We are on Canadian territory right now, and English is one of Canada's official languages, but not here in Quebec. Quebec governments have already passed laws against the English language without distinct society status in the Constitution. Imagine how much further they would go, and what a National Assembly with Lucien Bouchard at the head of it would do, with a distinct society clause in the Constitution. They would use it to absolutely diminish the rights of their minorities, and of anglophones, so much so that even more would leave, and then guess what they would do next: they would have another referendum.

So we'd accomplish nothing. That's why the lamb lobby is so incredibly dangerous, because by going along with distinct society, they are feeding the notion that right now Canada isn't good enough for Quebec.

That is exactly what the separatists are saying, when in fact, right now, Canada is terrific for Quebec. It has been a buffer zone to protect it against the rest of North America, and that's why Quebec hasn't ended up being quaint like Louisiana. Canada has fought constantly for the French language. And what sort of payback does it get? Bill 101 and Bill 178.

If the rest of Canada knew how stupid it was considered to be by the nationalists in Quebec, it would be outraged. Ontario contributes a billion dollars more into the unemployment insurance pie than it takes out; Quebec takes out a billion dollars more than it puts in. So, in effect, Ontario workers are subsidizing Quebec workers to the tune of a billion dollars a year, and have been for years. Thank goodness they still haven't figured out that if Quebec separates, there's a billion dollars for them immediately in terms of the money saved from equalization payments.

Canada has been compassionate and generous enough to send billions of dollars in equalization payments here each year, and in return, never mind a thank you, the popular mythology in Quebec is that Quebec subsidizes the rest of Canada! The vast majority of sovereignists are under the impression that Quebec sends more money to Ottawa than it gets back. So not only is there no gratitude; there is the impression that *Canada* is not grateful enough for all the money that Quebec sends!

Now, it's impolite to mention any of this, and, indeed, there would be no reason to mention it if not for the fact that the separatists use mythical arguments such as these to pave their way out of Canada. Mythology is what drives separatism, and until someone stands up to contradict the mythology, the separatists have us all on their playing field.

Far from being outraged, though, the elites who dominate this debate and tell us to support Plan A are veritable gluttons for punishment.

Characteristics of a Plan A Supporter

A Plan A supporter is one who feels we've just never done enough. Whatever's wrong, it must be our fault. If only we did more, then everything would be fine.

This is like the deluded husband, whose wife has left him, has told him she can't stand his guts, and has taken a new lover. He says to himself, "Well, perhaps if I bought her roses. I know what I'll do, I'll cook her dinner." So he goes out to get a recipe book to help him cook a beautiful dinner to save his marriage, while his wife is at her boyfriend's house. Think what good this recipe book would do. Absolutely none.

The situation in Canada has gone way too far. We have bent over backward, we have made all the concessions, but this Type A person has never met a concession he didn't like. The more he gives, the better he feels. This is the type of person the separatist likes to deal with. What you do with a Plan A person is this: you take a big basket, gather up all their concessions, say thank you very much, and then say, "You know what? Dammit, it's still not good enough. We're leaving!" And then the Plan A person will say, "You know, we didn't do enough."

It's a harvest of more and more concessions, and it has gone on for so long that when any Canadian actually dares to suggest an alternative to Plan A — when he says, "I'm not giving you any more presents" — the separatists are absolutely shocked. *Plan B?* The instant Plan B came up, they were utterly stunned by it. Until October 30, 1995, the vast majority of Canadians had been Plan A people — that was the view encouraged by the political elite. The average Canadian couldn't figure it out. He wondered to himself, "Why are we doing this, it never seems to work. But I guess our leadership thinks it's okay, so it must be." Since that time, though, people have begun to realize that if we keep following our leaders, we're going to walk right off the edge of a cliff.

Among the grass roots in Canada, the more people hear about Plan A, the less support there is for it. It's mainly the political elite and the chattering classes who try to sell everyone on it, those who would do well in any case, the millionaire property owners who believe in socialism provided it's not their wealth that's being taken. These are the people who know they could get good jobs no matter what, and who want to ingratiate themselves with the separatist regime. They're the ones who think that Plan A will work.

Yet even suggesting Plan A immediately validates the separatist argument that there's something wrong with Canada. For the average French Quebecer, the proof of this is that Canada keeps sending Quebec something to fix it. In other words, supporters of Plan A are the repairmen. If there's a repairman in the house, something must be broken.

If you're a federalist, you're certainly not going to win any friends among nationalist Quebecers by promising them distinct society. All you will succeed in doing is encouraging a culture of complaint among the soft nationalists, who, like spoiled teenagers, always want more freedom. Like teenagers, they want their independence, though without any harsh consequences. Isn't this what they've been encouraged to expect by the separatists?

And, like teenagers, they tend to blow any perceived slight out of all proportion. Consider the bitter complaint of a woman who phoned in to my talk show recently. She said she thinks the voter fraud which took place during the 1995 referendum is bad, but she's more concerned with the fact that a number of business leaders in Quebec sent out letters to their employees saying that if they voted Yes they'd be fired. This is intolerable in a democracy, she claimed.

The truth is it's *very* tolerable in a democracy, just as it's tolerable for unions to send out letters telling members how they should vote. Because neither the unions nor the bosses will know how their members or their employees voted in any case, because it's a secret ballot. To compare a letter suggesting how somebody should vote to *stealing* a vote and to suggest that they are the same thing indicates ignorance.

In the summer of 1996, a Canadian Airlines flight attendant was reprimanded for saying something technical to a small group of his colleagues in French. The next day, of course, I heard the usual hue and cry from a separatist caller. "This proves," the caller said, "that the French can't get served in their own language throughout Canada."

Of course, it proves nothing of the kind. Every Canadian Airline flight attendant, when stating the safety instructions, has to do so in both French and English — even if there's not a single francophone on board. That's what this country has done to make francophones feel that they are full partners in Confederation. Here's a case where one administrator adopted a stupid English-only policy in certain isolated situations when the crew is talking among themselves, and it's a typical example of how a minor mistake by one person in one company gets blown up into a situation of total turmoil — and, of course, justification to break up a country. Because some idiot administrator said you can't say a sentence in French to one disgruntled employee on one aircraft on one airline, Canada is therefore a terrible place. This is an example of how Quebec nationalists blow isolated incidents out of all proportion.

Now, the fact that separatists are using this argument is understandable. The fact that members of the lamb lobby buy it is unacceptable, because I have never yet been on a plane anywhere in Canada where the safety instructions weren't stated in French and in English. And how does Quebec respond to Canada's largesse and spirit of reasonable compromise? Well, safety instructions on Quebec roads are not printed in both of Canada's official languages. They're printed in French only. I guess it doesn't matter if English-speaking people have an accident.

When I asked my caller if he had ever been on a Canadian Airlines flight where safety instructions were not stated in French as well as English, he said he doesn't travel by plane.

People such as these callers, who are viscerally responsive to separation because of any perceived slight, are not in need of more concessions, because short of making the rest of the country unilingually French, they won't be satisfied with anything Canada does. What these people are in need of is a reality check. But all they get from the federal government and the lamb lobbyists is more grovelling.

Damage Control

The federal government has plenty of evidence that appeasing Quebec nationalists will not work, but, alas, they persist. Never underestimate the incompetence of politicians. Distinct society is a bad idea and Jean Chrétien knows it and so does Stéphane Dion, but now that they've been tricked into making that promise before the last referendum, they have to do something about it.

We discovered on October 30, 1995, that politicians can indeed be very stupid. They made a ridiculous promise, and now, in order to save face, they have to pretend that they believe in something, and to sell something that is both useless and unsaleable. They are buying into the separatist rhetoric, in effect saying, "You're right, there is a problem in Canada. It isn't good enough for you. We know why you're complaining. It is bad, and we have to fix it." This is a losing proposition, because the separatists don't want anything fixed within Canada.

Federalists instead have to say, "It *isn't* bad, it's *great*; we *don't* have to fix it, we *won't* fix it. This is the way it *is*, and the way *out* is extremely complicated." Once they say this, then the status quo would have more appeal.

It should be noted that the status quo isn't really a status quo, since Canada is constantly evolving. It should also be noted that in Quebec opinion polls, most Quebecers don't like the status quo. Many of them have no idea what it means, but they have been told they don't like it. That has to be changed, and the way to change it is to expose the separatist mythology for what it is. Instead of this, though, people like Chrétien and Dion and Daniel Johnson and Jean

Charest, in continuing this futile attempt to get Quebec recognized as a distinct society, are only adding to the damage that they've done so much to cause.

Now what they *should* do immediately — as soon as possible — is stop the bleeding. There's damage already, and that can't be undone. The federal government should never have made their promise to the Quebec Liberals. All they can do now is control the damage. They need to say to the Canadian people, "We may have thought this concept was a good one in the past, but we will not continue to sell it because 1) the people of Canada do not want it, and 2) even if they did, the government of Lucien Bouchard wouldn't accept it. The people of Canada, from coast to coast, voted it down in the referendum on the Charlottetown Accord. And while the Tories made the mistake of adopting the resolution at Charlottetown to begin with, we will not adopt the exact same damn stupid mistake."

They can say, "Yes, we did try to sell it, and we've since changed our minds." And the way to do it, in terms of winning PR points, is by saying, "We have changed our minds because the public knows better than we do. Millions of Canadians in the West don't like it and millions of sovereignists in Quebec don't like it. We now know that this is not the solution for anybody."

Now, Canadians may not like distinct society for different reasons. It's like a vase: you don't like it because it's too big, I don't like it because it's too small, but we can both agree, we're not bringing this vase into the house.

The federal government must get to this damage control quickly. Think about it: What more could a separatist want than for all the federalist leaders, in preparation for the next referendum, to be busy *not* thinking about the reality of what might happen after a Yes vote, but thinking only about distinct society — something that is unsaleable, and which would not change anything even if it were sold?

Impossible, you say? Unacceptable for a government to break such an important promise? Well, it's hardly unprecedented. Let's not suddenly get all self-righteous about how governments have to follow through on all their promises. Pierre Trudeau has shown us that what you run on and what you do are two different things. In the 1970s, the Conservatives, led by Robert Stanfield, proposed the adoption of wage and price controls. Now, who in their right mind would vote for someone who's going to take away your money? So the Liberals said, "We would never do that," and then soon after they got in they passed wage and price controls.

The current Liberal government has already broken a major promise over the GST. Who in their right mind would vote for a party that added 7 percent to the price of everything that you ever bought? No one. That's why the Conservatives were reduced to so few seats in Parliament that they could have a caucus meeting in a phone booth. The Liberals said they'd get rid of the GST. What happened once they got in? They kept it.

And what has happened to their popularity because they lied to the public? Absolutely nothing. As I write this, the Liberals are still at 57 percent support in the polls. So, breaking another promise will only hurt them with separatists who would never vote for them in the first place. The federalists must say they will not force "distinct society" into the Constitution since millions of Canadians, federalists and separatists alike, do not want it.

They have a tough choice to make. They can continue to lie to the public about something they know won't work, or they can be honest, admit to their error, and say they've changed their mind. They have done this in the past and they can do it again. But for the sake of preventing this country from being torn apart, what the Liberals must do is *stop pretending* that they're trying to sell distinct society when they know as well as we do that it can't sell.

Limit the damage. Don't give Lucien Bouchard the ammunition he needs just before the next referendum. Tell the public, "We passed it in the House of Commons, and the Bloc Québécois voted against it. We know that Canadians are united on many things, and one of the things they're united on is that distinct society is a useless expression that will not help anyone."

Be Prepared

Following the narrow victory by the No forces in the last referendum, the people of this country came to the shocking realization that the federal government had been completely ill-prepared to deal with the consequences of separation.

The separatists had worked hard and were prepared for either a Yes or a No vote, but unfortunately the same could not be said for the federal government. Had there been a narrow vote in favour of the Yes side, it would have been all over for this great country. Headlines around the world would have read, "Birth of a Nation." There would have been a near immediate unilateral declaration of independence in the National Assembly. The separatists would have called the shots, and there is absolutely nothing a stunned and unprepared federal government could have done about it.

That's what happens when the federal government and the leader of the No forces in Quebec, along with many members of the media elite and the chattering classes, engage in a conspiracy of silence by refusing to address the issue of basic ground rules for what would happen in the event of a Yes vote. The separatists were smart enough to make use of the federal silence and represent it as proof positive that a humbled federal government would go along with whatever the separatists dictated.

Is this what the people deserve from their federal government? Of course not.

But there was one very positive aspect of the October 30 referendum. You don't know what you have until you almost lose it. Canadians suddenly learned that they love this great country much more than they had realized.

They also came to another shocking realization. As children are growing up, they are convinced that their parents are in control and that they know what they are doing. However, there comes a time in childhood when a parent says or does something that makes the child realize that the parent does not know everything. That news, which almost always comes as a shock, is a defining moment in childhood.

For many Canadians, that defining moment came on the night of October 30, 1995, when they suddenly realized that Canada had barely survived an attempt to break it apart, not because of the federal government, but in spite of it.

That sudden realization is the reason for the spontaneous appearance of dozens of grassroots organizations all across Canada representing hundreds of thousands of Canadians, who now know that their federal government had no clue about what to do. The sad truth is that, while the separatists did indeed have everything under control, our federal government did not.

That must not be allowed to happen again.

Plan B: Reality Check

We're so used to the appeasement policy of Plan A, that Plan B is considered extreme. We've let the separatists go unchecked for so long that now it is considered hardline to stand up for Canada. And the truth of the matter is that Plan B is not about threatening Quebec or "getting tough" with Quebec. It is simply about presenting Quebec with a reality check — one which says, "Let's see what the situation really is, and what we can really do about it."

The C.D. Howe Institute has already drafted what it calls the "10 principles of Plan B," some of which are more specific than others. Whatever the government decides to adopt as its own set of ground rules, though, they should be in keeping with the four following reality checks:

1. Does everybody hate this country? *No*, twenty-eight million people love it. (There's a big shock right there.)
2. Are francophones oppressed? *No*, they *run* the country. (These are the shocking facts.)
3. Does one region of the country have the right to decide the borders for the entire country? *Of course not.*
4. Should a separatist sympathizer be the only one who counts the votes? *Of course not.*

These are the reality checks that are so important to look at. Step back from them for a moment, and you'll see how truly sensible they are. We're so used to the debate in Quebec that we tend to forget that there is not a single other jurisdiction on this planet that permits one region to have a referendum on secession, formulate its own question, and ask the question as often as it likes until it gets the answer it wants, all the while undermining the country as a whole. Canadians must not let spineless politicians like Jean Chrétien turn this country into the laughing stock of the world by allowing itself to be broken apart without so much as a whimper of protest.

Lucien Bouchard and the separatists cannot steal Canada away from millions of loyal Canadians. And they cannot rob Canada of millions of its loyal citizens who do not want to leave.

Let's not discuss this issue when it is too late. Let's discuss it right now. The longer the federal government maintains its silence on issues like partition and the illegality of a unilateral declaration of independence, the easier it will be for the separatists to perpetuate the myth that Ottawa will go along with whatever it says. That is a disservice to Quebecers because the truth of the matter is that in the event of a Yes, the people of Canada will not tolerate two Quebec politicians, Jean Chrétien and Lucien Bouchard, sitting down together to preside over the breakup of Canada.

Enough is enough. Stop wasting time on Plan A by trying to renew federalism for the sake of people who couldn't care less and whose only true goal is the destruction of the country that is the envy of the world. We must stop trying to beg people to like Canada as if it were some dud of a product that has to be mended before it becomes acceptable. Canada is not a losing proposition.

Canada is a gift. It is a great land of freedom and opportunity that has allowed English Canadians, French Canadians, and new Canadians to thrive, despite the constant threat of separation that has held us back and caused so much suffering for so many people.

The people of Quebec must finally be presented with a stark choice. On one hand, they are welcome to stay in Canada and continue to work together as we have for the past 130 years, in order to make this country even greater than it is already.

That is one choice. The other choice — the *only* other choice — is to join the separatists and work to break up Canada in order to set up an ethnic French state supported only by nationalist francophones.

Take the Separatists at their Word

While the separatists are the ones who want to destroy this country, at least we know what they are doing, because, to give credit where credit is due, they have been open and up front about it. The PQ did not deny that it was a separatist party. As a matter of fact, they sent millions of pamphlets to every household in Quebec openly stating that in the event of a Yes vote, they fully intended to turn Quebec into a separate country whether the rest of Canada liked it or not. Nothing subtle about it. Nothing hidden. They fully intended to issue a unilateral declaration of independence unless Canada agreed to their demands within one year or sooner as determined by the whim of the separatist-controlled National Assembly.

Since we know that the separatists have every intention of using a unilateral declaration of independence against the wishes of Canada and against the wishes of half of its own population, we must do everything in our power to prevent that from happening. We must not tolerate Quebec nationalists getting away with the largest land grab in Canadian history and taking millions of loyal Canadians along with them for the ride into chaos and confusion.

The Canadian government must show respect to the seven million Canadians who live in Quebec by telling them the truth about the real and immediate consequences they will have to face in the event of a vote for separation. Separatists are not the only people who have rights. All Quebecers have the right to have all the facts on the table.

Contingency Legislation

The terms of separation will not be dictated by Quebec, but neither will they be dictated by Ottawa. The two sides will attempt to reach a reasonable compromise. Once the federal government has put forth what it views as reasonable ground rules for the next referendum, then the separatists can review them and argue their case.

Will the debate be bitter and divisive? You bet it will be, but at least all Quebecers will finally realize that the breakup of a country is not a painless process wherein Quebec nationalists make all the decisions with the rest of the country nodding its head and saying, "Yes, sir." Let the debate take place in the House of Commons, where federalist members of the Liberal and Reform Party can argue it out with the separatist members of the Bloc Québécois in front of the entire nation. After they have argued, debated, and discussed, then they can move on to a democratic vote to pass contingency legislation on what has been debated.

That way, instead of taking a journey into the unknown, Quebecers will know exactly what they can expect the day after, the month after, and the year after they vote to break up this country. Perhaps they will realize that it just would not be worth it to go through all those complications simply because the federal government has intruded into a few provincial jurisdictions. Then again, perhaps they will decide to have their own country despite all the complications. In that case, so be it, but at least we will all be prepared, and nobody will be buying a pig in a poke.

The government of Canada has flirted with the idea of Plan B. They hint at it and then they back away. That is not enough. Plan B must be placed on the public agenda as soon as possible to be discussed in advance, while the situation is still calm and not at the last possible moment in a referendum campaign when it will be seen as nothing more than a campaign tactic.

In the throne speech of February 1996, the federal government vaguely promised that Canadians would have some kind of say in the future of their country. Vague promises are not enough. Of course Canadians must have a say in the future of their country. To do otherwise is to hand ourselves over to the dictates of self-obsessed nationalists who want to destroy what all of us have worked so hard to build.

Needless to say, the separatists will not be enamoured of Plan B. So what? We are not enamoured by the goal of the separatists to break up a country that is loved by 90 percent of its citizenry. Of course the separatists do not like Plan B! They do not want the people of Quebec to realize just how unpleasant and complicated it will be to achieve sovereignty. The separatists would much rather have the federal government preoccupied with such Plan A non-starters as distinct society, which a man with the rhetorical talent of Lucien Bouchard can easily dismiss as too little, too late.

Timing is of the essence. The federal government must immediately make it clear that it is *not* the National Assembly that will decide the future borders of Canada and it is not the National Assembly that will decide the future of millions of Canadians who have democratically indicated that they do not want to live under the shackles of a rogue regime established via an illegal unilateral declaration of independence.

The sooner the better. And, by the way, be prepared for the separatists to be not only provoked, but also quite surprised. They are used to fighting a one-sided battle where they do all the talking and set all the rules. They are not used to the federal government actually doing something to prevent the country from being dismantled by a dishonestly counted answer to a trick question.

The Opponents of Plan B

Conditional federalists have used a number of different arguments to get Canadians to abandon Plan B. One argument is that it will be counterproductive. It will only provoke the soft nationalists and encourage them to rally to the separatist cause. Rubbish. If they did not rally the last time when there was literally no risk to voting Yes — precisely because the federalists were so unprepared — they are certainly not going to join the separatists when they see all the risks they will encounter. If, on the other hand, Canada does not stand up for its interests, the separatists will win by default. They would win not because they have a great vision of a future independent Quebec. They would win not because separation is a good idea. They would win because Canadian politicians did not have the guts and the determination and the leadership qualities to stand up for Canada.

Thus far, misguided politicians and members of the lamb lobby are still hoping that if you do not pay attention to the separatist movement it will go away. They don't want you to even talk about Plan B because that might make it into a self-fulfilling prophecy. That argument is a load of hogwash, and the next time it is presented to you, ask the naive soul who has suggested it whether he or she has a smoke alarm in the house. If they do, then ask them to remove it immediately, since they certainly would not want it to become a self-fulfilling prophecy. Being prepared for a hurricane in a hurricane zone does not mean that you are hoping for a hurricane; it merely means that you are smart enough to be prepared for any eventuality instead of running around like a chicken with its head cut off at the last moment while the hurricane does its job.

Some misguided souls have had the temerity to suggest that even discussing Plan B is somehow unpatriotic. Because you would be jeopardizing this country's future, they reason, you are not being a true and loyal Canadian. *Au contraire.* To avoid discussing the topic is to play right into the hands of the separatists. They use the silence of the federal government by presenting it as clear evidence that Ottawa is offering tacit approval of whatever harebrained schemes the separatists concoct to fool the people into embarking on a disastrous adventure that the vast majority of them have clearly rejected time and time again.

But perhaps the most outrageous of all these arguments is the notion that, somehow, supporting Plan B is anti-French. That is an absolute lie, but cynical politicians will use it to discredit anyone who doesn't go along with their appeasement plans.

For instance, the Reform Party took an excellent stand on Quebec before the 1995 referendum, setting about twenty conditions of separation, outlining what might happen in terms of territorial arrangements, etcetera, and that's what the federal government should have talked about then. Had they done so, the vote would have been 60-40 in favour of the No side, because it would have frightened off a lot of the soft nationalists. The government, however, didn't do that.

Unfortunately, the Reform Party is not gaining any credibility in Quebec because it has been successfully depicted by the Liberals and the Conservatives as being anti-French, which is utter nonsense. *It isn't anti-French; it's anti-separatist.* There's a huge difference. There are millions of francophones in Quebec who are also anti-separatist. You don't hear a peep about that. Many of them, prominent figures such as Laurent Beaudoin, Paul Desmarais, and Claude Garcia, spoke out during the last referendum, even though it was politically incorrect to do so. The problem is that not enough of them spoke out. Jean Coutu, owner of the pharmacy chain that bears his name, spoke out, saying that the language laws are part of the problem, as is the chronic uncertainty in Quebec. These people, many of them highly successful industry leaders, realize what the separatists are doing to Quebec. They're anti-separatist; they're not anti-French.

But the separatist movement has been so successful because the separatists go completely uncountered. They appropriated the Quebec flag and now pretend that they own it. And they also created the ridiculous notion that to say No to any of Quebec's demands is anti-French. This is highly effective in preventing any kind of opposition, of course. If you are anti-sovereignist, you are considered an enemy of the Quebec people. Wrong! Half the people in Quebec are anti-separatist. Three and a half million people. These facts should be repeated again and again.

Who are the opponents of Plan B? The conditional federalists and the lamb lobby, of course.

Failed politicians like former Ontario premiers David Peterson and Bob Rae and Conservative Party leader Jean Charest have been sucking up to Quebec nationalists for so long for their own interests that they just do not know how to stop.

David Peterson once told me on my open-line radio program in Montreal that if I don't like the language laws in Quebec, I should pack up and leave. Strangely enough, that was precisely the same advice I had received from a racist separatist caller who would dearly love it if every anglophone moved out of La Belle Province.

I have no intention of taking the advice of either of those two esteemed gentlemen. This is my home, and I'm staying. For a wealthy lawyer like David Peterson, anglophones losing their rights in Quebec may be a small enough price to keep Canada united.

The problem is, it won't work. The separatists are no longer content to oppress their minority. The rest of Canada gave in too easily on that one. Now they have bigger fish to fry. They want to wear and tear Canada apart and start their own country where they can pass all the racist laws they want, all under the politically correct guise of protecting the French language and culture. What a pity that so few people have had the courage to point out that protecting one language does not mean undermining the rights of people who speak another language. Any country that is ready to sacrifice the rights of one million of its citizens isn't worth saving.

But I have a far deeper faith in the honesty and integrity of the Canadian people than I do in self-centred, failed politicians like David Peterson who have done enough damage already.

Far worse than David Peterson is Jean Charest. For some reason, many people in Quebec are convinced that he is the Captain Canada we need to save this country.

It may be true that Jean Charest is young and energetic, and he does have more charisma than Jean Chrétien or Daniel Johnson. But that's hardly enough. His corny pull-out-the-passport routine during the last referendum may have encouraged federalists and put them in a better mood, but it didn't accomplish much else. First of all, the over-whelming majority of Quebecers do not even own a passport, so they couldn't care less about the issue one way or another — especially when the federal government never said that it would deny Canadian passports to the citizens of a separate Quebec. The Canadian government never said it would deny *anything* to the citizens of a separate Quebec, and that is precisely why so many voted Yes the last time.

And while we are daydreaming that curly-locked Jean Charest will be the man who will save Canada, we keep forgetting that he could not even convince the people in his own riding to vote No. The people in Jean Charest's own riding voted to separate, and we think that he is the man who can talk Quebec nationalists out of separating? Let's get real.

Charest comes with the Conservative baggage of Brian Mulroney. He still believes in the failed initiatives of Meech and Charlottetown. Not only is he wedded to the notion of distinct society, he has gone even further: he has gone on record as saying that it is the very cornerstone of his Quebec policy. How out of touch can you get?

Brian Mulroney made a deal with the devil when he allied himself with Quebec nationalists to win the federal election. We are still paying the price for all the separatists he brought with him into the federal government. Jean Charest cannot even learn from Mulroney's mistakes. He, too, figures he can score a few seats by cozying up to the nationalists. The man still does not get it. If Quebecers want to vote for a nationalist, they will vote for the real thing: the Bloc Québécois. Why should they vote for the opportunistic, pseudo-nationalists of the Conservative Party who would only muddy the waters?

Charest has a right-wing platform that will alienate Quebec voters, and he is committed to pushing distinct society which will alienate the rest of Canada. How's that for a policy destined for disaster?

Forget about renewing federalism. Federalism is fine. It is separatism that is the problem, and not only does Jean Charest not have the solution, Jean Charest is part of the problem. For his own selfish interests, Charest, who is as power-hungry as any politician, is ready to risk the future of Canada.

Plan B is the only possible way to save Canada, but Charest publicly fights against it at every opportunity so that he can score points with Quebec nationalists. As recently as late June 1996, Charest has said that he will never put his name to any plan that allows for the partition of Quebec because he equates it to a death warrant for the nation. Don't believe this man for a moment. He has it all wrong. It is the separatist movement that would be the death warrant of Canada. And as for Jean Charest refusing to put his name on anything, fortunately for us all, that's irrelevant, and so is he.

As for the Liberals, Prime Minister Jean Chrétien is too busy on trumped-up trade missions to stand up against the separatists for more than twenty-four hours at a time. And no one in his cabinet seems to be any more prepared to come out unequivocally in favour of Plan B.

Take Sheila Copps, for example. This woman is surely one of the most cynical politicians in Canada, and she takes the Canadian people for complete idiots. Copps is not in favour of any reality check. Instead, she prefers to sell Quebecers on the merits of Canada by hawking flags and promoting the advantages of staying in Canada.

Gee, what a great idea! How come we never thought of that? Just tell Quebecers that Canada is a great country and we have nothing to worry about.

Yeah, right.

Copps is still so happy about having succeeded in shafting her own constituents that she seems to have forgotten that this kind of mindless nonsense is what brought us to the brink of disaster the last time around. It's time to stop wasting time telling Quebecers what they get if they stay in Canada and start drawing them a clear diagram about what they get — and more importantly what they do not get — if they leave.

Voting Provisions

To begin with, Plan B cannot allow the separatist movement to set the question on its own, because the answer will affect not only Quebec but the rest of the country as well. And we know full well the type of questions that the separatists like to ask. They want to make the question as confusing as possible because that is the only way they can fool enough people to go along with them on their foolhardy exercise. The separatist movement is not interested in an honest question. It is interested in a winning question.

Needless to say that when Quebec nationalists are told in no uncertain terms that the question that will radically affect all of Canada has to be decided by Quebec in conjunction with the representatives of the rest of Canada, they will be miffed. Separatists are always miffed. That's their job. They will say that Canadian participation in deciding the wording of the question means that the rest of Canada is interfering.

Let them say it. The separatist movement of Quebec has certainly interfered enough with the rest of Canada by ignoring the democratic wishes of the Quebec people to stay in Canada and further undermining the economy of the province — and the entire country — by threatening to have as many referendums as they can in order to get their way.

Plan B must also prevent Quebec from supervising the vote on its own, especially in light of the voter fraud that deprived tens of thousands of citizens of their democratic right to vote. We would have to be insane to leave the very future of Canada as we know it in the hands of Quebec Chief Electoral Officer Pierre F. Côté, a man who thinks that unreported bus rentals are more dangerous to democracy than blatant voter fraud. In the next referendum, we must have UN observers present to monitor the vote count.

Costs and Consequences

Every piece of news that indicates that separatism is complicated and filled with risk lessens the support for independence. Here is what must be put forth in Plan B as the consequences of a vote in favour of sovereignty:

1. **You are voting to have Quebec become a separate country.**

There will be no economic partnership, and there will be no political partnership. We will continue to trade with you as we do with Sweden, but there will be no economic partnership.

Quebec can use Canadian currency so long as it wishes; it will have no say, however, in the Bank of Canada. The Bank of Canada will continue to set interest rates and do whatever it wants with no Quebec members, no Quebec input, and no Quebec suggestions, just as we don't listen to what Sweden says.

But if Sweden would like to use Canadian currency, that's fine. Barbados uses American currency, but no one in Barbados sets American interest policy and fiscal policy. In like fashion, yes, you can use the Canadian dollar, but the interest rates will be set for you by Ottawa.

2. You leave with what you came in with.

You do not take what doesn't belong to you. That includes 3.5 million people who do not believe in your government, who do not believe in the way you've conducted the referendum, who don't believe in the way you've counted the votes. And, as Canadians, these 3.5 million people are our responsibility, so we're going to have to negotiate what to do about this.

As well, we will have to negotiate what to do about certain amounts of territory that were given to Quebec as a province. Quebec's territorial boundaries are protected and can't be changed without the consent of the National Assembly *while Quebec is a province*. When it is no longer a province, it is game over.

To suggest that the boundaries of Canada can be changed by 10 percent of the population without one peep out of the other 90 percent is an incredible absurdity. There is no precedent anywhere else on earth where 10 percent of the population decides to rearrange, redraw, and re-mark the boundaries of an entire country, and the other 90 percent have to shut up while this is going on.

Now, when people hear that the day after a Yes vote, the first thing on the agenda will be territory, then when they're voting Yes, they'll know that they're not just voting for a flag party the next day; they'll know they're also voting for an ugly, bitter, divisive debate. And they'll know that this debate is a natural outcome of separation.

Coming to Terms

Plan A supporters tend to regard any such talk as threatening to everyone, because, they reason, the separatists won't take kindly to being given an ultimatum. But, once again, they have it completely backwards. It's the separatists who are saying, "After we vote Yes, we will tell you what the deal is. And if you don't accept our terms, we are going to separate unilaterally. It's none of your business, one way or the other." *They're* the ones giving the ultimatum.

I'm not suggesting we give Quebec any ultimatum whatsoever — only a reality check which says, "Here are the facts. Now go ahead and vote. Vote Yes or No. And if you vote No, this is the deal you get: you are not going to hijack the country, the extortion is going to stop. And if you vote Yes, that's fine. Then we will discuss passports, citizenship, territory. You appoint your people to do the negotiating for you, we appoint our people and we'll take however long it takes. We'll all suffer in the meantime. Canada is not a prison; we're not keeping you against your will, but you're not taking everything with you."

Deep down, most rational Quebecers understand that the situation cannot go on as it has been. When the issue of partition first came up, *La Presse* columnist Lysiane Gagnon wrote a column titled, in English, "Over Our Dead

Bodies." A few months later, though, she was talking about the outcome of a Yes vote, and she conceded that there would have to be lots of negotiations, including territory. Well, if negotiating territory is not partition, I don't know what is.

How will it end up? Will Sherbrooke Street East become part of Quebec or remain part of Canada? I have no idea. But there will be serious negotiation. There's no way around it, and by putting forth Plan B, the government will not be waiting until after a Yes vote, when the country is in chaos and we're all screwed from coast to coast. Have all this discussion, negotiation, and debate in advance.

Where? In the House of Commons. Democratically elected separatists and democratically elected federalists representing the two schools of thought in Canada can sit and debate these issues. And they will be ugly and bitter and divisive debates, but it's better that these debates take place in the calm of the House of Commons than on the streets.

Partition

Partition is the logical outcome of separation. There are going to be some jurisdictions that want to leave Canada, and there will be some that want to stay.

No outside forces need be involved. The Canadian army certainly doesn't need to come in. What would happen is that the 3.5 million federalists in Quebec would simply say, "This is part of Canada. It was part of Canada yesterday and it's part of Canada today."

Now, what is the government of Quebec going to do to prevent Montreal from saying it's still part of Canada? What's to stop Montrealers from saying, "You can make all the declarations in the National Assembly that you like, you can declare you're part of California if you like — what you're doing is against the law, we're not joining you in what's against the law, and that's it."

It all depends on who can establish control over the territory. Canada already has control, so it doesn't have to do anything. The people who want to change things are the separatists in the National Assembly. And how are they going to do that? Start shooting fellow Quebecers? The first shots that they fire, they would immediately become a rogue republic, recognized by no one in the world — not even France. They can't shoot their own people. So, what is the National Assembly going to do?

Violence would be counterproductive for everyone involved. If there were rioting in the streets, international investment would grind to a total halt. Quebec would become the latest hot zone in the world. The United States would not stand for this kind of situation on its borders, which raises the possibility of the Americans getting involved by sending in the marines as peacekeepers, with the aim of keeping the two sides apart, as they've done in other parts of the world.

None of this would be pleasant, of course. But to say that, because a few people might riot, we should hand over Canada on a silver platter doesn't make any sense. The argument of the lamb lobby is, "Give them what they want or they're going to get angry." What I'm saying is if you do that you are teaching them to continue to get angry and that they will get more. I'm saying that enough is enough, let them get angry. We will not be terrorized out of our country because some people are angry.

Polls have shown that if there is any violence, support for sovereignty would plummet. There is no support for that kind of violence, because there's not that kind of oppression. Even if the Canadian army were to come in, it would be strictly in a peacekeeping role. They would no more be inclined to shoot at fellow Canadians than Sûreté du Québec officers would be to shoot at fellow Quebecers, whether federalists or separatists.

This is my entire point. I think we have a peace-loving country, and I think that the thirty million people of Canada are peace loving whether they're anglophone or francophone, federalist or separatist. And that's not going to change if Canada decides to stand up to Quebec. We're not doing anything different than the separatists are doing. They're presenting their point of view, and they have a right to do that; we have a right to present our point of view. Just because they say they're going to divide up Canada whether we like it or not does not mean we have to accept it.

During the 1995 referendum, Daniel Johnson managed to keep the issue of partition off the table, so that it was not discussed — not in the newspapers, not on radio, not on TV, not in the debates, not in any of the campaign literature. That is absolutely remarkable, because it is the most natural outcome of separation. Yet the Liberals and the PQ and the media all managed to keep this issue off the table. There was a conspiracy of silence.

Fortunately, that's over. They can't do this anymore. It *is* on the table, it's going to be discussed, and they can no longer hide it. Bouchard's talked about it, Johnson's talked about it, Chrétien's talked about it. Now, let's get together and we'll talk about it a hell of a lot more when it comes closer to the next referendum. That's how people can make an informed decision.

As for any potential instability, we have to worry about those possibilities. I guarantee you that federalists are worried about them and separatists are worried about them. Neither side wants to see the situation turn violent. Because that's a lot worse than the current situation, from anybody's point of view. So I think everybody will work together to prevent that scenario from happening.

Separatists are no more rabid than anyone else. The ones in Lac-St-Jean who dislike the English — they've never met anyone who's English, they just hate them from two centuries of mythology — they're seeing the rest of Canada come around to allowing Quebec to be separate, but not allowing it to have the same territories. Now everyone's going to have to put a little water in their wine.

If and when partition comes about, it's not going to be the way I would have liked it to look, and it's not going to be the way Lucien Bouchard would have liked it to look. It'll be some kind of compromise. It's all a matter of minimizing the number of unhappy people. But to say that once you separate we will not bring up partition, and to say that every single anglophone will go along with separation, is a lie.

The Threat of Violence

There are two kinds of response to the partition of both Canada and Quebec: the kind that is legal and the kind that is illegal. The legal response involves both sides having a civilized discussion over various legal territorial claims. Whether it's in Ottawa or Quebec City, or whether it's on the border or bridge between Ottawa and Hull, there will be a civilized discussion.

The alternative to civilized discussion is violence. And I really don't think separatists are any more interested in violence than are federalists. I doubt that there is anyone in Canada who would like to trade in this magnificent, peaceful country for a war zone. I certainly don't think that we should be racist and suggest that separatists are any more prone or any less prone to violence than federalists.

Consider the average Yes voter. Let's say she's a single mother with two kids, a proud Quebecer who's bought all the mythology that Ottawa is evil, that Quebec subsidizes the rest of Canada, that they're oppressed, that they've been conquered. She voted Yes in 1995, and I can understand and sympathize with her. Why not, after all? There were no consequences laid out for her to consider. Now, when she hears these discussions, when she sees her federal MPs in Ottawa and her representatives in Quebec City holding these discussions having to do with partition and violence, she's going to be less interested in voting Yes in another referendum.

One side isn't more interested in violence than the other. There are a bunch of hotheads in each group who will have to be dealt with by the authorities. But the overwhelming majority of Yes voters are just like the overwhelming majority of No voters: they want this to be settled in a peaceful, civilized manner. And for us to think only of the few hotheads and to twist the country around in order to suit them is insane.

The vast majority of Canadians are freedom-loving, law-abiding people who aren't interested in violence. It is precisely when the FLQ arrived, and people saw that someone like Pierre Laporte had been murdered, that the movement lost support. Support for sovereignty plummeted because of that one act of violence. Why? Because the overwhelming proportion of Quebecers — separatists and federalists alike — do not want to live in that kind of environment. Their oppression from Ottawa simply does not exist, but even for the ones in whose minds it does exist, it is not the kind of oppression that requires a violent solution.

Quebec is a peace-loving society. There have been polls showing that Lucien Bouchard's vicious attack on Chrétien during the 1995 referendum — that nasty one where he depicted the prime minister as a traitor — did not play that well across Quebec, and that it lost the separatists some overnight support. People were afraid of this kind of demagoguery. The people of Quebec have great respect for the tradition of freedom, and they've always had this freedom in Canada. And they got a little bit nervous watching their leader foaming at the mouth, just as they got a little bit nervous about Jacques Parizeau's comments against ethnics and calls for revenge.

A Unilateral Declaration
of Independence Is Illegal

Plan B must clearly state that a unilateral declaration of independence from the National Assembly will not be recognized by the government of Canada. More and more, separatists are being challenged on this point, as people realize that this sort of threat has no place in a democracy.

Quebec City lawyer Guy Bertrand is a former founding member of the PQ, who changed his tune when he saw that this country allows separatists into the House of Commons, even though they're committed to the breakup of Canada.

When he saw this, he said to himself, "How democratic can you get?" He looks around and sees there's not another country on earth that would allow this. Canada is so democratic that it allows separatists to become members of parliament, treats them with all the respect due to MPs, and allows their leader to become the leader of the official opposition. Bertrand thought to himself, "We've been badmouthing this country for being anti-democratic, when it is incredibly democratic." So he became a federalist, and one who is not afraid to stand up to his former party (he knows the separatist mentality inside and out). He filed a court case against the Quebec government, which, he maintains, does not have the right to deprive millions of Canadians of their rights under the Charter.

The PQ doesn't want to hear about this and neither do

the Quebec Liberals, because they want to stay in this state of mythology where Quebec can do whatever it likes and the rest of Canada has to shut up. That is the picture they've painted, and they don't want anybody marring that clear picture. *We do what we want, we shaft the rest of Canada, they sit still, and that's it.* In his court case, Bertrand says that the federal government *has no choice* but to intervene in the event of a unilateral declaration of independence by Quebec. Now, if the Canadian government had stayed out of this case, it would have been doing what it did last time. It would be going along with the separatist viewpoint. The government had no choice but to say, "If there is a breakup of Canada, we would have to be involved in the discussion." And when Bouchard heard this, he immediately flew into a rage, which he does very easily — that's his specialty — and threatened to call a snap election and referendum.

Chrétien did it anyway. Bouchard called an emergency cabinet meeting, and — poof! — there was no emergency, Bouchard backed off. There's no snap referendum, no snap election. He backed off completely.

That's the key thing to remember. If you allow the separatists' lies to go unchallenged, you ensure that the lies will continue, and that they will be that much more difficult to counter in the future. Don't be afraid to challenge the separatists and call their bluff. These are people too cowardly to even ask a direct question on the referendum ballot. When the going gets tough, the nationalists back off big time.

PART 4

SURREALISM IN QUEBEC

Politics in Quebec these days is truly characterized by the bizarre. Grown men and women, well-clothed and educated, stand up in the National Assembly or tell the media here that anyone who is against their separatist option has to remain "neutral" in the national unity debate.

Case in point:

In one of Jean Chrétien's few inspired moves to date, he decided to name Jean-Louis Roux as the new lieutenant governor for Quebec. Roux is a critically acclaimed and well-loved Quebec actor, who also happens to be a staunch federalist, and who has said publicly that in the event of a Yes vote he might leave Quebec.

The separatists are naturally quite upset that now they are faced with this prominent French Quebecer who has said that nationalism can lead to intolerance. Furthermore, no Quebec law can be passed without him signing it. He can't sign a unilateral declaration of independence, because then he'd be signing himself out of a job. After all, he'd be abolishing the monarchy, and he's the representative of the monarch in Quebec. Doing so would cause a constitutional crisis, and he isn't likely to do it.

Upon Roux's appointment, Lucien Bouchard immediately said he doesn't want him interfering in the sovereignty question. He wants him to remain neutral. Bouchard is highly selective, of course. Roux's predecessor, Martial Asselin, was also supposed to remain neutral, yet he had no problem saying that, in the aftermath of a referendum, Quebec should be recognized as a "people." This was direct interference, but, of course, it was perfectly acceptable to the separatists because it perpetuated their myth. And a myth it most certainly is. Who are the "Quebec people"? Are anglophone federalists part of the Quebec people? Are francophone Quebecers who are federalists part of the Quebec people? Ask them. They'll tell you No, they're part of the Canadian people. The native peoples — are they part of the Quebec people? Certainly not. So how dare someone like Martial Asselin make this kind of suggestion?

All of a sudden, the representative of the federal government and the Queen in Quebec has to stay neutral as the separatists go about dismantling the country. The lieutenant governor *can't* remain neutral on this issue. But then, Bouchard's comments here are perfectly in keeping with the basic premise of the sovereignty movement: My mind's made up; don't confuse me with the facts.

Consider the example of Richard LeHir, a sovereignist who is now sitting in the National Assembly as an independent. LeHir was commissioned to do studies on separation, and he was told to make sure the studies show that separation works. (They certainly don't want studies that show that it doesn't.) So, he does his job, and he comes up with studies which show that, for the most part, it works, but even he and the separatists can't find studies that show that breaking up a country is a wonderful idea and that we'll all thrive. And some of the results are negative. They're not in keeping with the sovereignist mythology, and in Quebec, when it comes to mythology versus logic, logic gets thrown out the window.

The studies basically said, "This is our option. It is going to cost something, and this is what we found will be the cost. Do you want to go for it? We feel it's worth it, but this is what it's going to cost." Lucien Bouchard throws out LeHir's documents, and the results of the studies disappear with his magic wand in one sentence. He says, "These are not my studies."

Anywhere else, journalists would say, "Who cares whose studies they are? They were legitimate studies and they say it doesn't work as smoothly as the separatist politicians are all saying. Let's look at them." Not in Quebec, though. They disappeared from the news within twenty-four hours.

In Quebec, most of the francophone press are in their twenties to forties and are staunch sovereignists. They go along with the party line. After all, they have been taught by their professors, who are baby boomers, who grew up in the age when they thought that Quebec was a colony of the rest of Canada, and a place where all French Canadians were badly treated by the fat lady at Eaton's.

The list of fun quotes that go unchallenged by the press could fill a humour book. Unemployment in Canada slips down slightly to under 10 percent. In Quebec it skyrockets to 12.4 percent. More jobs lost, month after month. It's clear to anybody that it's the political uncertainty causing this economic stress. What does Lucien Bouchard say? "No it isn't. It's the global trends."

The global trends apparently don't affect Toronto, and they don't affect Vancouver or Calgary or Winnipeg, but they do affect Montreal. *La Presse* tried calling the unemployment figures "A Disaster" for Quebec, but the other story on the same page was that Jean-Louis Roux might cause a constitutional crisis as the lieutenant governor, and the media's attention went off in that direction, leaving Bouchard's remarks unchallenged. When Bouchard doesn't blame Quebec unemployment on global trends, he blames it on the weather. Once again, I am not making this up.

When the Quebec government looks at the issues of unemployment and the economy, they can't handle them. Why? Because *they're* the separatist government that is causing the problem in the first place. They're the ones who are causing the lack of employment and the the lack of investment. So what do they do to take people's minds off the misery caused by the unemployment? What do they do to blind them to the fact that there are all these For Rent and For Sale signs, and that the economy is going to hell in a handbasket? Well, they start spreading preposterous notions such as *Montreal is still not French enough.*

It used to be that every nationalist in Quebec couldn't get service in French from the fat lady at Eaton's. Well, the fat lady at Eaton's now has a friend in Montreal: a nurse at the Jewish General Hospital. Here's how the story goes:

A French Canadian journalist named Normand Lester has a heart attack, and winds up in the cardiology unit at the Jewish General Hospital. His heart stops, but the doctors save his life. The doctors and nurses at the hospital speak to him and his wife in French only for nine days. And they save his life. So far so good.

Then, when he's in recovery, he's speaking to a nurse voluntarily in fluent English and asks her for something that she can't do because, she says, she doesn't have permission. Suddenly, apparently angry because his request has been denied, he tells her not to address him in English, that she must address him in French. Meanwhile, he had been speaking to her in English up to this point. She gets upset at him and does something she shouldn't have. She asks him to speak in English. Later, she sends him a formal letter of apology.

Lester nonetheless goes to the press with this letter of apology, and it makes the front page of *La Presse*. Does he mention the first nine days he spent in the cardiology unit, where they not only saved his life, but spoke to him in French only? No, he leaves that out. Instead, he paints a picture of this nurse yelling at him, saying, "You're in an English hospital, you have to speak English." This causes an outrage, of course. It's taken to mean that it's worse for francophones than it's ever been before. And the entire mythology is recreated.

Is the Jewish General Hospital unilingually English? Of course not. Fifty percent of its staff are francophone, and everyone who works there can speak in French. This man, whose life was saved, *was* served in French. But that wasn't the issue for him. He's a journalist, and he has a political agenda, which is to "prove" that French is endangered — when it is not. But you need this to perpetuate the victim mythology, to justify why this is an ethnocentric government that is more concerned with the interests of one group over another.

But there is humour to this. L'Office de la langue française — an organization paid for by the taxpayers of Quebec to spy to make sure businesses have all the right signage, and who can come into your office and ask to look at your internal documents to see if they're in French — is conducting an inquiry to find out if anglophones are discriminated against. This organization, which was established under the pretence of protecting the French language, undermines the English community and diminishes its importance, and is now in charge of examining whether or not there's any problem of discrimination.

That's like asking Mila Mulroney to look into the Airbus scandal. Their credibility level on this is less than zero. Their purpose is not to find out if there is discrimination against anglophones. Obviously, they will come to the conclusion that there isn't any. Discrimination is precisely their agenda. The conflict of interest is so blatant, it's ridiculous.

We're faced with this day in and day out in Quebec. And

it is going from bad to worse. Until now, the elderly or those on welfare paid nothing or only two dollars per prescription for their medication, with the Quebec government subsidizing the rest of the cost. Now, the PQ has introduced a new drug insurance plan that is going to cost everybody a whole lot more money, scheduled to go into effect on January 1, 1997. But they jumped the gun on the elderly. For some reason, their costs jumped as of August 1, 1996. Does the government care about the votes of the elderly? Of course not. The vast majority of the elderly vote No.

Why do the elderly tend to vote along federalist lines? Because they're more conservative, and naturally more worried about the possible fallout from separation. Someone who is elderly tends to be less of a dreamer who believes that everything will work out effortlessly and that there will be no problems. They've lived a full life, are aware that there can be problems, and are much more realistic than sixteen-year-olds would be.

Did someone say sixteen-year-olds? Some members of the PQ, in their effort to do anything possible to win, have suggested lowering the voting age to sixteen. You heard right. If the referendum is in three years, that would mean the fate of this country would be voted on by kids who are now twelve or thirteen years old, who are now busy in school learning that Canada is the root of all evil. How do you think they're going to vote? You don't need to be a rocket scientist — or a political scientist, for that matter — to figure that out.

And who would protest? The PQ brings it up for a vote in the National Assembly. *Should sixteen-year-olds have the right to vote?* The PQ has seventy-seven seats, the Liberals have forty-seven. *Next.* And Canada has no say in it. *None of your business.*

Just how surreal are the arguments of Quebec separatists? Pierre Bourgault, the same man who warned of a reaction against anglophones in the event that they cause Quebec separatists to lose the referendum, actually wrote that minority rights would be better protected in an independent Quebec. That's right. Apparently, a sovereign Quebec would be more self-confident, less paranoid, and therefore more generous in giving back rights to the English-speaking minority. There need then be no repressive sign laws. We could have all our rights back again.

Pierre Bourgault has a great future in comedy, and he should definitely try out for the next Just for Laughs festival in Montreal. He can do the shows in both French and English.

What people don't seem to understand is there are hundreds of thousands of Quebecers who have no intention of living in the French state of Quebec. They're attached to Canada. They don't care how warm and friendly or cold and unfriendly this new government is, they want to live in Canada. So a Quebec government would have to deal with that reality, and it would be a harsh reality.

The purpose of separation is to turn Quebec into a French state. Jacques Parizeau, who is far less radical than Pierre Bourgault, has said he thinks there are too many English-language radio stations in Quebec already.

The separatists may whine incessantly that the French *language* is in danger, but it is the English *community* in Quebec that is in danger. The English language will survive no matter what. But if the ethnocentric racists who dominate the PQ have their way, the English community will disappear. Slowly but surely, their institutions will close, their schools will close, their hospitals will close, there will be fewer job opportunities for them, and they will eventually leave.

And then, the French language and culture will still be unprotected, because Quebec will still be surrounded by a sea of anglophones. All that will have been accomplished is that the separatists will have succeeded in erasing the inconvenient fact that English-speaking Canadians helped build this province.

The most hysterical part of the mythology in Quebec is the notion that anglophones are the best-treated minority in the world. Among the arguments is that we have all these wonderful institutions like McGill University and the Royal Victoria Hospital and the Montreal General Hospital and the Jewish General Hospital. What the separatists don't mention is that these were not all part of some magnanimous gift; these institutions were built by the English-speaking community. Our "generous" provincial government tried to erase our language from public view, though their own courts prevented it. The good and kind government has refused to allow immigrants to attend any of our schools, thereby guaranteeing that the number of students will dwindle, leading the schools to eventually close down. It is almost impossible for an anglophone to get a job in the civil service of Quebec or even in the municipal government of Montreal, with very few exceptions.

And the tragedy of it is, you don't even have to wait to get refused. Most anglophones are so convinced of the institutional prejudice against them, they don't even bother to apply. Young, talented English-speaking students graduating from McGill or Concordia wouldn't *think* of submitting an application to a Quebec government department even though they're fluently bilingual, because they figure they wouldn't even be looked at anyway. And in many cases they're right. All it takes is some racist bureaucrat to throw out the application, or the fear of a racist bureaucrat — the very perception makes all the difference.

One caller to my radio talk show related an anecdote about a computer company that had contacted a Quebec government department and explained that they had confirmed orders from Albania, Romania, and other countries from the former Soviet bloc for some computer programs developed by them here in Montreal. They were asking the government for some export help. For seventeen months, the department placed in charge of this by the Quebec government ignored them, didn't respond to them because the letter was written in English. Finally, the company got fed up and it moved thousands of jobs with this project to Plattsburgh, New York. Now, this has to do with one or two sheets of paper of an application, one or two bureaucrats in the Quebec government, but the result is thousands of jobs lost. There is a direct connection between the racist language laws and the racist language attitude by members of the Quebec government, and the sorry state of the economy in Quebec. And this is just one example. There are many more.

What is most frightening to people here is that the state has the right to marginalize one group of its citizens. The state has far too much power in this province, and the reason people are so upset about the sign laws is that they are an example of the state interfering with the law of the marketplace, with the rights of people, and showing a preference for one group of its citizens over another. That is what has terrified a lot of people from all walks of life — English and French, rich, poor, and middle class — and convinced them to leave Quebec. They are sick and tired and frightened of the state intervention that is not the will of the people at all. The language hardliners and racists are a minority, but unfortunately, they're the government of the day. And Lucien Bouchard is no exception. He's the one who made the comment about the white race. He's the one who said Montreal should not be bilingualized.

The Cost of Uncertainty in Quebec

The fact that 300,000 Quebecers have left the province over the last twenty years is more than a mere statistic. They took with them tens of millions, if not hundreds of millions, of dollars in spending power. They're not buying merchandise in Quebec stores, and they're not paying taxes to Quebec. And that makes matters worse. If those 300,000 people had not been scared away by the spectre of separation, the economy here would be doing a lot better because there would be 300,000 more customers for whatever goods and services are being sold in the province. It is an incredible tragedy that has been foisted upon the people of this province by their separatist government.

Families are being torn apart, though I guess that means Bell Canada's doing all right, since the long-distance lines are buzzing as families try to keep in touch with one another. But this chronic uncertainty is how communities disintegrate. And they didn't disintegrate on a whim. The people who live in Ontario don't worry that all of their children have left and gone somewhere else. Nor do the people in B.C. This is a problem exclusive to Quebec. 300,000 people have not left any other province. This is the greatest mass migration in Canadian history, and it is because of the racism that is inherent in the separatist movement.

And it's all so sanitized. The separatists have perfected the art of destroying communities and coming off smelling like a rose. If there's an ethnic group you want to get rid of, don't lift a finger against them. Just pass restrictive language legislation that the federal government is too scared to stop, and the people will slowly but surely leave. A few more referendums, a few more graffiti-scrawled walls saying "Anglo Go Home," make sure you don't hire any of them in the civil service, make it virtually impossible for young anglos to get a job — eventually, more and more of them will leave. On their way out, they'll pay for their own moving expenses, and their departure will help lower the price of houses, so it will be easier for others to buy them. You don't even have to go to their institutions to close them. They'll put on the padlocks themselves, because as people leave their communities, those left behind won't be able to maintain their schools. They'll close the schools, they'll close the hospitals, and the fewer institutions they have, the less desire the people have to stay. The younger generation leaves, the parents perhaps go to where their kids are, and so they get rid of themselves on their own, and the government still has a sterling international reputation. It didn't lift a finger. The people left on their own.

Once the separatists wear enough of their opponents down, once most of them have already left, well, then it would become a homogenous French country, wouldn't it? So much for the warmth Pierre Bourgault says anglos would receive in that case.

And the separatists talk about how open and tolerant they are. Theirs, we're told, is purely a linguistic struggle, having nothing to do with race or ethnicity. Well, isn't it strange that nobody votes for this option unless they are *pure laine* Québécois. The number of anglos and ethnics who vote for it is infinitesimal.

Even French ethnics aren't voting for it, yet they speak perfect French. And how many Moroccan Jews are in the Quebec civil service? Zip. Nada. They speak French pretty well from what I hear, and yet they don't get into the civil service. How many Haitians or Vietnamese francophones have been deemed worthy enough to "fit in"?

Whenever separatists make a racist comment, the lamb lobby rushes to their defence, saying, "They don't really mean what they said, these are just isolated incidents." Well, these isolated incidents come from the premier, the deputy premier, the former premier — they come from the leadership of the separatist movement. These aren't some isolated drunks in a tavern who made these comments; these are the leaders of the movement.

PART 5

WHAT ABOUT THE REST OF CANADA?

I've said elsewhere that turning back the tide of separation won't be easy, and it certainly won't happen overnight. But I do hope that we get our act together soon, before it's too late.

Canadians do not possess limitless generosity, and there is a growing tendency within the rest of the country to say, "To hell with the separatists, let 'em go." I only hope that we will be able to persuade the federal government to do what it should do to stand up and prevent the destruction of our country, before the people in the rest of Canada figure out how stupid they've been.

Not only have Canadians put up with the separatist threat, but they've actually been subsidizing the separatist movement. The Canada Council is reported to have actually funded a study on separation. You're simply not going to find any other country on the planet whose federal government funds a study on how to break itself up.

But there is evidence that the rest of Canada is finally starting to wake up.

How the West Can Finally Win

There is a separatist movement in British Columbia that is starting to take off. It isn't really all that serious, though it has climbed from 12 percent support to 15 percent support in a very short time.

It's not based on ethnic nationalism, so it isn't as powerful as the separatist movement in Quebec. But it is based on the sense of alienation many western Canadians feel, and the belief that Ottawa ignores B.C. What this movement demonstrates is that the people in British Columbia are finally realizing that the way to get Ottawa's attention is by threatening to leave. If you don't do that, the federal government will ignore you completely. Now, the separatists in British Columbia are new at the game, so there's plenty they can pick up from the sovereignty movement in Quebec.

To begin with, after having whipped up sufficient popular resentment against the federal government, hold a provincial referendum in which you ask the people to vote on a trick question. Don't ask, "Do you want British Columbia to become a separate country from Canada?" The question should be, "Would you like the provincial legislature in British Columbia to have more jurisdictional powers while maintaining an economic and political association with the rest of Canada?" From 15 percent support today, support would zoom up to 50 or 60 percent easily, because the voters would be unaware that the question had to do with separatism. Then, of course, once the vote was in, it would be too late.

Next, the B.C. separatists should conduct feasibility studies on sovereignty. Then, once the studies come in, throw out the ones that suggest it may not work out so well. When talking to the media and the public, refer only to those studies that show separation is not only painless, but downright necessary.

As well, it is extremely important for the B.C. separatists to state up front that they'll hold as many referendums as it takes until they get a Yes vote. Oh, and a No vote doesn't count. A No just means that there will be another referendum; a Yes vote is final.

It is also crucial, of course, that a very good friend of the founder of the B.C. separatist movement become the chief electoral officer for life. Then, have him count the votes and grant him the final say in whether or not there was any voter fraud, if it is revealed that there were thousands of spoiled ballots.

And, finally, don't forget: Tell the rest of Canada that all this is none of their business.

Now, it sounds preposterous. It's straight out of a comedy skit, right?

It isn't.

It's exactly what the sovereignists here in Quebec did during the referendum of October 30, 1995, and the reason people didn't laugh here is because, when there was no response from the federal government, it became accepted wisdom that somehow these shenanigans are acceptable.

The End of Canada?

Some might suggest that support for separation in British Columbia indicates the Canadian federation is already on the verge of collapse, that Canada is not a viable country, not worth saving.

But that's a distortion of the situation. The separatists in B.C. don't think Canada is not worth saving. They are simply fed up with paying for the rest of Canada while being ignored. And the noise that these separatists are now making will likely have the same effect that the sovereignty movement in Quebec has had.

Whenever Quebec has threatened to separate, they've gotten more and more concessions from Ottawa. If B.C. got all of the perks that Quebec did, there would be no separatist movement whatsoever in B.C.

The difference is the separatist movement in Quebec is not here because the separatists want more perks or more jurisdictions; the separatist movement here exists because a group of ethnic nationalists wants to create a French country in North America, where the interests of one linguistic group are placed above the interests of every other linguistic group. That is not the purpose in B.C.

If there is a devolution of powers from Ottawa to the provinces — if, for instance, the federal government stops destroying the coastal fisheries and the coastal towns of British Columbia — the provinces are satisfied, and wouldn't even contemplate separation. If Ottawa gives in to B.C., B.C. is happy. If Ottawa gives in to Quebec, it doesn't make one bit of difference. Because the separatist movement in Quebec has nothing to do with controlling *more* jurisdictions; it has to do with controlling *all* jurisdictions. They want the kit and caboodle. The Allaire Report, commissioned by an allegedly non-separatist government, proposed what basically amounted to separation with equalization payments.

The difference between the two movements is that, by and large, Quebec separatists hate Canada. Out west, the separatists don't say they're British Columbians first and then Canadians; they say they're Canadians first and they live in British Columbia.

When British Columbians were polled on the issue, the question was, "Are you in favour of thinking about British Columbia as a separate country?" Eighty-five percent of British Columbians have no intention of even *contemplating* separation.

Now, it's one thing to be in favour of *thinking* about

something. I'm in favour of flying to the moon, for instance, but I have no intention of doing it. So, they can be in favour of thinking about separation, but if this was a week or two before an actual referendum in B.C., I don't think they'd even have the 15 percent. It isn't even an organized movement. It is, however, a way to complain, and they see how well Quebec has done by using this as a threat. This country is not falling apart. People in Saskatchewan are very proud to live in Saskatchewan, but they're also very proud Canadians. There are proud Canadians in every part of the country, including Quebec, except for two million separatists who are not proud Canadians, who hate this country because it has been presented to them as evil incarnate.

The Narcissism of the Separatists

Separatists in Quebec either haven't given any thought to the fact that there are millions of other Canadians who would be affected by the breakup of their country, or they just don't care. They're so consumed with their own sense of self-importance, that they take it as their right that they can do whatever they want to do.

This is intolerable. Say I live in a co-op apartment with a dog. I can have a democratic vote in my second-floor co-op apartment and ask myself and my dog if we would like to have a big explosion, because we like loud noises. The question would be, "Should we have a big explosion in the apartment?" and I could get a 100 percent vote on that. As for my upstairs and my downstairs neighbours, it's none of their business. That would be an intrusion into our democratic decision.

Now, of course, in the event of an explosion the upstairs and downstairs would be damaged, and so my neighbours would want to have some input in the whole matter. And the same situation holds true for the entire national unity debate. Quebec separating from Canada has an impact on every single Canadian, so every single Canadian has to be involved.

The counterargument I'm presented with is, "Well, Quebec isn't moving anywhere, it's going to stay in the same place." That's true, but one region cannot change the borders of the rest of the country without the rest of the country having some say in the matter, because what you would have is a country split in two. Canada's border would start at British Columbia and continue to Quebec, where it would stop. Then, after hundreds of miles, the country's border would start again at the Maritime provinces. And to think that Canada would go along with this without any debate, without any discussion, is preposterous and outrageous.

I think the vast majority of Canadians in the wake of the 1995 referendum are asking themselves, "Why is this going on? Why do the separatists get to do this and there's no contradiction from the federal government?" Then, alone in the privacy of their living rooms or in their kitchens they think, "You know what, I must be wrong, I guess the politicians must know better." But slowly we're realizing the politicians do *not* know better, and that the success of the separatist movement is due almost entirely to lack of opposition. That's why it's been so successful.

PART 6

GRASSROOTS UNITY MOVEMENTS

If we are counting on our political representatives in Ottawa or in our home provinces to find a solution to our national unity crisis, we might as well pack it in right here and now.

The more they try to "manage" the crisis, the more it seems like nothing will ever change for the better. Canadians want the matter resolved once and for all. What has happened, though, is that many have already decided to bypass their politicians, mostly out of sheer frustration at the way they've bungled the whole crisis almost from the beginning.

The unity groups which have sprung up all across the country are comprised of people who were stunned by the razor-thin margin of victory in the 1995 referendum. Watching the results as they came in, they thought to themselves, "You know what? I thought the politicians could handle it, and they can't. I don't know what I want to do, but I want to do something."

A lot of people thought the same thing at the same time. Before you knew it, each of them told a friend, who in turn told a friend, and they started all these different groups. At first, most of them were panicking and freaking out, not knowing what to do. But that's natural. It takes a while for these sorts of grassroots movements to gel. They should keep at it, and take comfort in the fact that they are part of a fast-growing movement that will bring Canadians from coast to coast closer together than ever before.

One of the more successful groups thus far has been the Quebec Political Action Committee, led by Howard Galganov, a Montreal-area businessman, which managed to unite some twenty federalist groups to support one simple cause: a boycott of major chain stores which refused to post at least some English signs to show a modicum of respect for anglophone customers in areas that are 80 percent English speaking.

The mere threat of a boycott was an unqualified success, and even inspired francophone groups in the Ottawa region and elsewhere around the country to adopt a similar tactic aimed at making their presence felt by stores failing to offer some French signs. These demands are perfectly legitimate, since Canada is a bilingual nation. And we should not shy away from this.

Why are these groups so important? Because for each person who's a member of a unity group, there are another fifty who would like to be a member. They didn't bother to join, but they feel the exact same way, and are losing trust in their politicians. In other words, the silent majority that all politicians strive to reach are now being represented by the unity groups.

It's not by coincidence that dozens and dozens of organizations are forming at the same time, all with different ways of approaching the same goal of keeping Canada together, and with the same feeling of frustration that the government couldn't do it. This level of frustration is unparalleled in Canadian history, and that's why the politicians are paying attention. Stéphane Dion even had a meeting with one of these groups. The purpose of his meeting, sadly, was to convince them of the nonsensical notion of distinct society. But the fact that he took the time to meet with them indicates that he felt they carried enough clout to be of some importance.

They are of extreme importance. It is through them, and only through them, that the balance of power will finally shift in this country from appeasement-driven conditional federalists to patriotic Canadians.

Now, this movement is still young, and as such is going through some growing pains. Many of the unity groups outside of Quebec are, for the moment, totally misguided. Maybe it's the distance. A lot of these groups seem to think that what Quebec is missing is *love*. It is the old Hallmark greeting card approach, and the same old distinct society gambit, which somehow these groups think are what will make the threat of sovereignty go away.

Jan Brown, the ex-Reform MP, is a perfect example of someone who figures that "more love" will do the trick, and on a person-to-person basis, it's great. She was the one who put the rose on Lucien Bouchard's desk in Parliament when he almost died from the flesh-eating bacteria disease that he had. This was very moving and very touching. Did it transform Lucien Bouchard into a federalist? Was he moved by all the get-well cards and by that yellow rose?

Of course not. He basically said, "Thanks for the lovely rose. I'm going to break up your country anyway."

Jan Brown wants to get attention. That's why she quit the Reform Party, that's why she placed the rose on Bouchard's desk, and that's why she took a special bus trip across Quebec this past summer to "get to know the people." As with any politician, she's motivated by her desire for a higher national profile.

Can she fix the situation in Quebec? No. She doesn't have a clue.

Her problem is the same as that of many of the unity organizations outside of Quebec. They simply do not understand who runs this province. They think they can go over Lucien Bouchard's head and express their love directly to the people, who will then be so taken with this gesture that they will turn around and join them in rolling back the separatist agenda.

That isn't the way it works.

It is the political elite who dominate the agenda in this province. What the unity groups have to offer Quebec *will not get through to the people*. It has to be filtered through the government, which is a separatist government, and that government is not interested in anything that smacks of national unity.

The proof of that is what happened in 1982. The people didn't mind the patriation of the Constitution; a separatist government at the time did. And for these same politicians, nothing has changed. They're not going to want to show that Canada works.

You simply cannot say you're going to ignore the National Assembly and go straight to the people. Because in Quebec, for some reason, the National Assembly is the only thing that counts. That's why language hardliners like Josée Legault are upset that some clauses in Bill 101 were rolled back by the courts. After all, separatists regard them as unelected judges thwarting the people's will.

Unity groups outside of Quebec are not helping the situation by telling the government to "go soft on Quebec." We've done that, and it hasn't worked. What Quebec needs is not more gifts or Hallmark greeting cards, and it doesn't need "tough love" either. What all Quebecers desperately need is a reality check, so they can make up their own minds once and for all.

And that's what these unity groups in the rest of Canada should be pushing for. When they talk to the federal government, via their local MPs or otherwise, they should say, "Make it clear the next time. Put a reality check into the next round of debates on sovereignty. Let's get serious about this. It could go either way, so don't toy with Canadians and Quebecers; let's explore what will be the consequences *now*."

If they hope to have the kind of clout in Canada that they could have, unity groups throughout the country must get with the times.

More and more Canadians are sick and tired of begging Quebec to stay. *We've gone through this for decades*, they are saying. *We've tried to bend over backwards with official bilingualism, with everything else, we've voted for one French Canadian prime minister after another, our currency is bilingual, we spent five times as much on francophone athletes as on anglophone athletes, we let them try to write seditious letters to the army, we pretend we don't mind.*

We've said, you can decide to break up Canada; we won't interfere. We've gone as far as we possibly can; we can't go any further.

And more and more Canadians are advocating the same message: give the people of Quebec — as citizens of Canada — the courtesy of a reality check. Don't treat them like children by not bringing up the serious consequences. There *are* serious consequences. Be honest, up front, and let them make an informed decision.

Because, let's face it, in 1995, the people of Quebec did not make an informed decision. When one-third of Yes voters thought that they would continue to send MPs to Parliament in Ottawa, they clearly had no idea they were voting for separation. They had no idea that they were voting to create another country.

These unity groups must also stop focusing exclusively on Quebec and consider what separation would mean for Canadians *from coast to coast*. They must contradict the notion — and it is unparalleled in history, with the exception of India — that you can take a country, break it into two separate parts, and in the middle of these two separate parts, place a foreign country, another sovereign entity.

That's a serious matter that hasn't been brought up; it has neither been debated nor discussed. What should be done about the St. Lawrence Seaway, for instance, in terms of protecting all the interests of Canada? What should be done to ensure that the Maritime provinces are not severed geographically from the rest of their own country?

These are the kinds of issues that have been brushed under the carpet, and that is precisely the reason the sovereignty movement did so well last time. Yet I was stunned to learn that people in British Columbia are very aware of partition, and support it. They do not want Quebec to leave with all of its territory, and it is crucial for Quebecers to know this before the next referendum. The unity groups would do well to make their feelings on these issues known to their political representatives.

The closer you are to the situation, it seems, the better you understand it. I think that most of the grassroots organizations in Quebec are doing exactly the right thing. They are pushing for municipalities within the province to pass resolutions stating that they wish to remain a part of Canada, no matter what kind of illegal declarations are made by the National Assembly. They've done this in the Pontiac, and they've got to do this in other regions across Quebec.

Once this happens, then the people of Canada will start to realize, "You know what? It isn't really just a bunch of separatists in Quebec. There are millions of federalists in Quebec who are really very proud of this country, and against all odds and despite what is politically correct, they are standing up for Canada. And we should stand up for them."

Jacques Parizeau blamed the referendum loss on the ethnics. Well, the ethnics can't do it alone. They can't keep saving Canada by themselves. They need our help.

And don't be fooled into thinking that next time it'll all be settled. Not under the current rules, it won't. Lucien Bouchard's said that if the next answer is No, he's just going to have a fourth, fifth, sixth, and seventh referendum until he gets the response he's been looking for.

At some point, Canadians have a right to ask their government to guarantee them some form of stability against a movement that is hell-bent on breaking up their country.

PART 7

CONLUSION: CANADA *IS* A REAL COUNTRY

Many Quebecers are finally waking up to the fact that their threat of separating has been taken seriously. They may have meant it merely to get more concessions out of Canada, but it hasn't worked, because the rest of Canada has taken them at their word, thanks to comments like Jacques Parizeau's statement that once the lobsters are in the pot, it's too late, and thanks to the letters of sedition from Jean-Marc Jacob to the Canadian army. Now Canadians in the rest of the country are saying, "You know what? These separatists aren't joking, they're serious. They want to have their own country, let's react to them in that manner." The thrust of their response is, "You may vote on your own future, but you are not dictating the terms to the people of Canada."

And the people need to make sure their government gets on board.

This is what a real country must do when confronted with separation. After all the cheesy references to the virtues of owning a Canadian passport, after all the UN studies telling us how fortunate we are to live in Canada, and after all the flag-waving, what the people of Quebec need to know are the true consequences of breaking up Canada. They need a reality check specifying what those consequences would be. They need a reality check, and anything less is doing them, as well as all Canadians, a disservice.

Yet this can never be the whole story. For Canadians are not a dour people, but an open-hearted nation, willing to help each other through the bad times just as we celebrate the good times. And sometimes it takes some pretty bad times indeed to show just how much of a caring nation we are and can be.

What happened in the Saguenay-Lac-St-Jean region in July 1996, with the devastating floods and subsequent outpouring of relief aid from throughout the country, proved what federalists have been saying all along: Canada is a great country because it consists of Canadians who are caring and compassionate, and who care for one another whether they live in British Columbia or Prince Edward Island. And the fact that the only time people in the rest of Canada ever come across the words Saguenay-Lac-St-Jean is when they hear them described as the "separatist heartland" didn't matter at all. In spite of politics, the overwhelming majority of people in the rest of Canada wanted to help out, from little girls who called up the Red Cross and wanted to donate their allowance, to community efforts in Newfoundland, in P.E.I., in Alberta, in Saskatchewan, absolutely everywhere.

Now, it's not a matter of what kind of compensation comes from the federal government, because that compensation goes to the Quebec government and the Quebec government issues the cheques. So people looking at where their cheques are coming from are still going to think it's all from Quebec. That's not the issue, and besides, those people pay taxes so they have the same right to the federal money as do people who are living anywhere else in the rest of the country.

The Saguenay-Lac-St-Jean relief effort will have a lasting impact on the national unity debate, though, because it was the first chink in the armour, the first step on the road toward breaking the mythology. It was the first successful way for Jean Chrétien to get to those nationalists, to prove that Canada does indeed care about Quebec. The picture of Canada as evil, of English Canadians as being hateful toward Quebec and Quebecers and wanting the worst for Quebecers, was disproven by all this fund-raising across Canada, and all this money coming in from individuals and corporations.

This is not the picture that sovereignists in Lac-St-Jean have been presented with. During the 1995 referendum, support for sovereignty in Lac-St-Jean was 75 percent Yes, 25 percent No. The 25 percent No supporters now have some ammunition. Now when they're discussing politics at the brasserie or the dépanneur, they can say, "Remember what happened when we had that disaster? There was money donated. Those aren't such bad people in the rest of Canada. They helped us. Not Ottawa; people, other Canadians in the rest of Canada."

Only the world's greatest cynic would refer to the outpouring of donations to the region from across the country as being politically motivated. Sure, the talk-show hosts and the politicians may have made a political thing out of it, but the girl who sent her allowance to the Red Cross after seeing the horrific televised images of people losing their homes had no idea about politics. She's not getting any political mileage out of it.

Will Lac-St-Jean become a federalist hotbed next time around? Certainly not. But will support for sovereignty ever reach 75 percent again? Never. It will never again go that high. Lucien Bouchard can't go any higher in that area, he can only lose ground, and my prediction is that the next time, the sovereignty figures there, instead of being 75 percent support, will be 60 or 65 percent. And I think that shift will be reflected in the rest of the province as well. The aid that came flowing in was part of a grassroots movement. It was human-to-human, person-to-person helping, and that message, I think, will get through to many people — not everyone, but many people — in Saguenay-Lac-St-Jean and in the rest of Quebec.

Let me tell you, when you're up on your rooftop and your house is being flooded, and a helicopter comes along and it's a Canadian helicopter, and it saves your life, that stays in your mind. Not only does it stay in your mind, but you tend to talk about it afterwards, and you wonder about your political options. And again, through word of mouth, things begin to change. It's not going to turn the picture around completely in Saguenay-Lac-St-Jean, but the important point is that *it will make a difference*. It will give the federalists in the region some material, something to say on Canada's behalf. What have they said in defence of Canada before that wouldn't have been shot down immediately? This is the first chink in the mythology that undergirds the separatist movement.

And, ultimately, that mythology must be replaced by the truth.

It is a myth that separatists can simply destroy Canada without the rest of the country being involved.

It is a myth that Canada has been, is, or ever will be a prison for Quebec, or a cemetery for the French language.

It is most certainly a myth that Canadians all over the country don't care passionately about keeping the country together, and making all Quebecers feel both wanted and welcome.

It is a myth that Quebec sends in much more than it gets back from Ottawa.

Most importantly, Lucien Bouchard put forth the biggest myth of all when he said that "Canada is divisible because Canada is not a real country."

We are a *very* real country, one which is routinely called the best place in the world to live. We are a pluralistic, multicultural, bilingual society which has had a wonderful history of shared power. At various times in our history, we've been governed by French Canadians as well as English-speaking Canadians. And with such a diversity of peoples living here, we have managed to create one of the most peace-loving, dynamic, open, and tolerant societies in the world.

We must expose the separatists' notion that Canada is not a real country for the myth that it is. If we fail to do this, we will almost certainly prove their point.

We must stand up for Canada proudly and unashamedly. Let us continue chipping away at the mythology and start presenting the truth. Because, as Mordecai Richler once said to the late Barbara Frum, "The truth is always in season."